creative
PICTURE
FRAMING

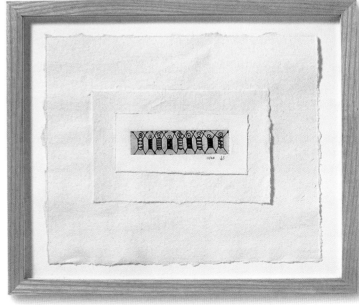

creative
PICTURE
FRAMING

A PRACTICAL GUIDE TO MAKING AND DECORATING BEAUTIFUL
FRAMES SHOWN STEP BY STEP IN OVER 450 PHOTOGRAPHS

RIAN KANDUTH

southwater

This edition is published by Southwater, an imprint of Anness Publishing Ltd, Hermes House, 88–89 Blackfriars Road, London SE1 8HA; tel. 020 7401 2077; fax 020 7633 9499

www.southwaterbooks.com; www.annesspublishing.com

If you like the images in this book and would like to investigate using them for publishing, promotions or advertising, please visit www.practicalpictures.com for more information.

UK distributor: Book Trade Services; tel. 0116 2759086; fax 0116 2759090; uksales@booktradeservices.com; exportsales@booktradeservices.com
North American distributor: National Book Network; tel. 301 459 3366; fax 301 429 5746; www.nbnbooks.com
Australian distributor: Pan Macmillan Australia; tel. 1300 135 113; fax 1300 135 103; customer.service@macmillan.com.au
New Zealand distributor: David Bateman Ltd; tel. (09) 415 7664; fax (09) 415 8892

Publisher: Joanna Lorenz
Editor: Elizabeth Woodland
Project Editor: Simona Hill
Copy Editors: Beverley Jollands and Heather Haynes
Designer: Nigel Partridge
Production Controller: Darren Price

ETHICAL TRADING POLICY

At Anness Publishing we believe that business should be conducted in an ethical and ecologically sustainable way, with respect for the environment and a proper regard to the replacement of the natural resources we employ. We are therefore currently growing more than 750,000 trees in three Scottish forest plantations: Berrymoss (130 hectares/320 acres), West Touxhill (125 hectares/305 acres) and Deveron Forest (75 hectares/185 acres). The forests we manage contain more than 3.5 times the number of trees employed each year in making paper for the books we manufacture. Because of this ongoing ecological investment programme, you, as our customer, can have the pleasure and reassurance of knowing that a tree is being cultivated on your behalf to naturally replace the materials used to make the book you are holding. For further information about this scheme, go to www.annesspublishing.com/trees

A CIP catalogue record for this book is available from the British Library.

Previously published as *Picture Framing*

PUBLISHER'S NOTES

• Wear protective gloves and goggles when cutting glass or wire. Wear a face mask when sawing, sanding or drilling medium density fibreboard, working with powdered grout or using solvent-based sprays.
• Although the advice and information in this book are believed to be accurate and true at the time of going to press, neither the author nor the publisher can accept any legal responsibility or liability for any errors or omissions that may have been made nor for any inaccuracies nor for any loss, harm or injury that comes about from following instructions or advice in this book.
• Before you begin any project you should be sure and confident that you fully understand the instructions.
• Levels of difficulty are indicated by a tool symbol, from one to three.

Contents

Introduction

If you've never tried making your own picture frames, you will be amazed at the transformation you can bring about. Even the most modest artwork or photograph can be magically enhanced by the imaginative addition of a complementary frame. Children will be thrilled at seeing their creations impressively presented, and you will have endless scope for making unique gifts.

Whether you are dealing with a dusty old painting, a mirror or simply a beautiful autumn leaf picked up during a country walk, framing is all about knowing how to combine materials and colour. Divided into two sections, the first part of the book, The Art of Framing, covers basic framing materials, equipment and techniques, including lots of step-by-step projects to help you gain confidence. The second section of the book, Paint Effects, deals with paint techniques and decorative ornamentation, and also features step-by-

step projects to experiment with and create.

You will learn about essential frame components – mounts and mouldings – and the many exciting ways to mount images, from a single-window mount to multiple and stepped mounts, and even shaped

mounts. You can use card or fabric, while the colour you select will influence the end result. There are dozens of decorative moulding styles to choose from, each profile capable of influencing the image in a subtly different way. In addition to ready-made moulding, you can also use lots of other materials – for instance, skirting board profile, pieces of driftwood or even self-adhesive lead strips can all be used creatively. Glass is good for preserving certain types of inset.

Paint Effects explores the many decorative treatments you can apply to frames. These range from simple painting and colourwashing through to more complex techniques. Here, you will discover the secrets of stencilling and stamping, distressing

and antiquing, liming wax and crackle varnish, and various gilding methods. You will also learn how to create unusual effects such as mock tortoiseshell, raised motifs, ink penwork, scorching and batik.

Picture framing is essentially about being as creative as you like. The book contains so many wonderful ideas that you will have plenty of frames to keep for yourself and lots to give away to friends and family.

The Art of
Framing

The ideal frame is one that effectively shows off the picture within it, whether that is a work of art, a photograph or the reflection in a mirror. It should not overpower the image or clash with its style. Careful choice is one of the most important skills in framing, and knowing what will work best is something that often comes with practice. This chapter aims to show you how to take everything into account and frame your pictures successfully.

Framing Facts

Although it may seem daunting to begin with, framing is actually not really difficult once you have decided on the style of your frame and worked out the materials you are going to use. Invest in the right tools and equipment from the start: they'll make framing easy and enjoyable and ensure that you produce results you are proud to hang on your walls. Although items

like a mitre saw and clamp may seem expensive, they are essential for perfect mitring and will enable you to achieve the absolute accuracy you need for a professional-looking result.

This chapter sets out all the basics of framing. If you are a complete novice, it's sensible to read through all the instructions and advice carefully before you begin. Even if you think you already know your way around a picture

frame, you'll find useful tips to help you refine your technique. The chapter begins with mounts (mats) – which can be just as important as a frame in making the most of a picture. Once you have learned how to make a basic mount, you can master the art of

making a stepped-window mount, multiple-window mounts for a set of pictures, a fabric mount and even shaped-window mounts. There are also some tips and ideas for effective ways to decorate a mount to show off a picture to its best effect.

Then there are step-by-step instructions for making the actual frames, from the basic shapes to the more unusual. Detailed illustrations show how to saw mitred corners, how to assemble a frame, and how to make the most of mouldings. You can also

learn how to create an unusual jigsaw-style frame, a multiple-window frame, a box frame, a cross-over frame and even a frame constructed from rustic driftwood. The art of glass-cutting is illustrated, with advice on the type of glass to use.

Finally, there are projects showing how to frame different sorts of pictures, whether they are oils on canvas, three-dimensional objects or even engraved stone, with some hints on hanging and fixtures. Armed with all this information, you can set about filling your walls with beautiful framed pictures.

Most of the items listed below are basic frame-making equipment, which you will use many times, so it is worth investing in any you do not already have. Specialist tools are available from framing suppliers.

Materials and Equipment

Acid-free hinging tape

Water-soluble gummed tissue tape is used to make tab hinges to secure artwork to a backing board. It should be weaker than the paper of the artwork so that it tears first if the assembly is broken up.

Blade

When cutting windows in mounts (mats) a blade is needed to release the cut corners to avoid tearing and give a neat, sharp finish.

Bradawl (awl)

Used for making initial holes in hardboard or wood.

Burnishing tools

A burnishing bone is for smoothing the cut edges of a mount (mat). The traditional gilder's agate burnisher is used to polish water-gilded surfaces.

Clamps

These come in all shapes and sizes and have various uses. A mitre clamp

is a metal fixture, usually bolted to a workbench, in which moulding lengths are cut at a 45° angle.

Corner gauge

When decorating mounts (mats), this fits into the corner of the window to allow pencil corner marks to be positioned accurately.

Craft knife

This has multiple uses in picture framing. There are several varieties so choose one that feels comfortable.

Cutting mat

Essential when cutting with a craft knife, as it protects the underlying surface. Self-healing cutting mats stay smooth and free from score marks.

Drill and drill bits

Both electric and hand drills are suitable for frame making.

D-rings

Picture wire is threaded through these for hanging. D-rings are available as single or double. Attach them to the backing board with butterflies (rivet-like fixings), or screw into the back of the frame.

Frame clamp

Frames are clamped to hold the joints together while the glue dries.

Framer's point gun

This specialist tool is used for fitting up picture frames. It inserts flat pins horizontally into the moulding to hold the backing board in place.

Glass cutter

Diamond-headed and tungsten types for heavy-duty glass cutting can be quite expensive, but cheaper alternatives are available for domestic use.

Glue

PVA (white) glue is used to hold the mitre joints in frames. Two-part **epoxy resin glue** forms a very strong bond for joining metal and stone. **Rubber solution glue** is used for attaching fabrics to mounts (mats).

Hacksaw

Used in a mitre clamp to cut wooden or manufactured mouldings. There are various types of blade, including blades for cutting metal mouldings.

Heatgun

Normally intended for stripping painted wood, an electric heat gun can be used to scorch patterns in wooden mouldings.

Mitre box

This two-sided wooden box has deep slots at a 45° angle to take a tenon saw for cutting moulding lengths. Its high sides keep the saw vertical and help to steady the moulding.

Mount (mat) board

The wide range of mount boards available fall mainly into two categories: regular and conservation. Regular boards are cheaper but the acid from the wood pulp used to make them will damage artwork over the years. Conservation boards are acid-free and will not damage artwork.

Mount (mat) cutter

A tool for cutting a bevelled window out of mount (mat) board. You can buy hand-held versions from good art stores and framing suppliers.

Paintbrushes

Use flat-face oil and sable brushes, approximately 1cm/½in and 2.5cm/1in wide, for detailing and pointing. Use stencil brushes for stencilling.

Panel pins (brads)

Thin pins are used for joining frames and tacking the backing board to the frame in the final assembly stage.

Safety gloves

Wear rubber (latex) gloves when painting, and protective cotton or leather gloves when handling metal foils or cutting glass.

Safety mask

Use with any paint or varnish sprays to avoid inhaling the mist, and when sawing MDF, which creates a large amount of fine dust.

Straight edge rule

Use for marking and cutting lines.

Tack hammer

A lightweight hammer is used for tapping in panel pins (brads); it can be used as an alternative to the V-nail joiner when assembling frames.

Tape measure

Used for measuring artwork, mounts and moulding.

Tenon saw

A 30cm/12in-wide flat saw used with a mitre box to cut wooden or manufactured mouldings. The reinforced upper edge keeps the blade rigid to allow very accurate straight cuts.

T-square

A measuring tool used to give a true square or rectangle. Used for marking up mounts (mats) and cutting glass.

V-nail joiner

When the frame is being joined together it is used to push V-shaped nails across the mitres to hold them together. It can also be used to secure the backing board to the frame.

V-nails

Used with the V-nail joiner to underpin the frame.

Wire cutters

Used to cut picture wire.

Wood

Mouldings are available in both soft and hardwoods in many designs. Those sold for framing have a ready-cut rebate to take the picture and glass. **Plywood** is an ideal material for making frames. It consists of thin sheets of wood glued together; the grains of wood in adjacent sheets are arranged at right angles to each other, which makes it exceptionally strong. It can be used to make backing boards as an alternative to **hardboard**.

A picture frame serves a dual purpose: it is designed both to display and to protect the painting or photograph within it, and all its various components contribute to these functions.

The Parts of a Frame

The component parts of the frame form a multi-layered sandwich, with the picture or photograph as the filling. The backing board, which is usually made of hardboard, gives rigidity. If delicate artwork is being framed, the backing board should be overlaid by an acid-free barrier to give extra protection. The image itself can be secured to the backing board using tab hinges of acid-free paper tape.

When a picture is to be displayed within a window mount (mat), it is customary to allow a slightly larger margin at the bottom of the mount than at the top or sides, to correct an optical illusion which occurs when the picture is hung on the wall. If all the margins were the same width, the bottom one would appear smaller than the others.

It is very important to take precise measurements before making a mount, and it is usually worth checking all your measurements before you begin to cut anything.

If a mount is not used, narrow wooden fillets should be inserted in the frame between the glass and the picture, to prevent the glass from touching the surface of the artwork. These will be visible when the picture is hung, so the wood should be selected to coordinate well with the image and the frame.

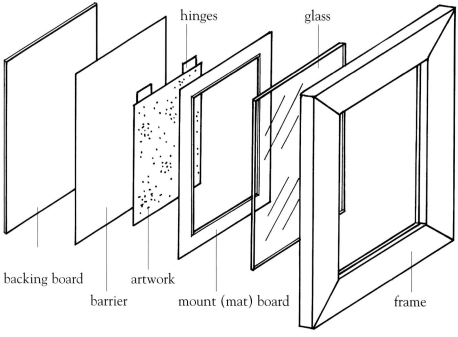

backing board   barrier   artwork   hinges   mount (mat) board   glass   frame

The mount (mat) keeps the artwork away from the glass. Paper expands and contracts with temperature and humidity changes, which can result in buckling. The mount allows room for movement in the artwork.

Single-window Mount

you will need

picture

mount (mat) board

tape measure

soft pencil

ruler

straight edge

mount (mat) cutter

cutting mat

blade

eraser

acid-free hinging tape

1 Measure the picture vertically and horizontally and add 7.5cm/3in to the top and both sides and 9cm/3½in at the bottom. You can now use these dimensions to cut the mount (mat) board to size.

2 Mark the inner measurements on the reverse side of the mount board using a pencil and ruler. Join up the pencil marks, crossing the lines so that you can see clearly where you need to stop cutting.

3 Line up the straight edge against the first marked line, push the mount cutter blade into the board and move it steadily along the marked line to cut out the window. Go over the pencil mark cross-overs only slightly, to avoid visible cross-cuts on the face of the mount.

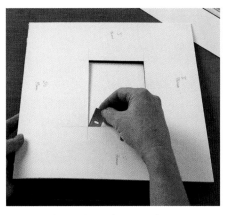

4 Cut the other three sides, turning the board so that you are always cutting vertically. Once you have cut out the window, carefully insert a blade into each corner and trim the edge to release the centre freely. This will avoid any tearing of the corners. Erase the pencil marks.

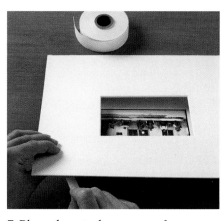

5 Place the window mount face up on the picture below it, and line them up. Attach the picture to the mount using acid-free hinging tape on the top edge of the artwork.

Use multiple-window mounts (mats) for collections of photographs or memorabilia that have a common theme, such as a series of old sepia prints, photographs of family members or a set of architectural studies.

Multiple-window Mount

you will need

pictures

mount (mat) board

soft pencil

ruler

T-square

mount (mat) cutter

cutting mat

blade

eraser

acid-free hinging tape

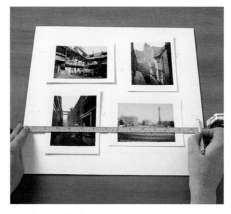

1 Place all the pictures on a piece of mount (mat) board. Using a ruler and pencil, mark the horizontal measurements of the two top and bottom pictures, just touching the pictures on all sides with the pencil.

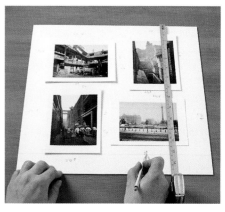

2 Next, mark the vertical measurements of the top and bottom pictures in pencil, again just touching the pictures on all sides.

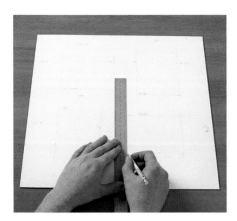

3 Once the measurements have been marked, join them up using a pencil and a ruler. Be sure to make crossovers, so when cutting the mount you will know where to stop.

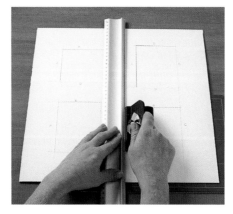

4 Cut out all the windows, cutting the left-hand side of each first, then the top, then the right-hand side, then the bottom. Move the mount board as you work, so you are cutting vertically. Erase the pencil marks.

5 When all the windows have been cut, position and hinge the pictures as for the single window mount.

This design is similar to a single window mount (mat) but with the addition of a second mount, with a slightly larger window opening, stuck on top. This results in an interesting stepped look.

Stepped Mount

you will need

tape measure

mount (mat) cutter

straight edge

cutting mat

2 pieces of mount (mat) board

soft pencil

T-square

blade

eraser

PVA (white) glue

glue brush

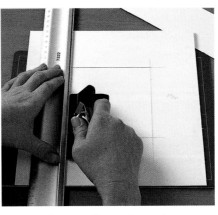

1 Measure the picture to be framed vertically and horizontally. Following the measurements, cut two pieces of mount (mat) board the same size, in proportion with the picture.

2 Mark the dimensions of the picture on both boards in the desired position. On one piece, draw a second line 1cm/½in larger than the original measurement on each side.

3 Cut the small windows from one board and the larger window from the second board using a mount (mat) cutter and blade and protecting the work surface with a cutting mat.

4 Erase the pencil marks and apply PVA (white) glue to the back of the larger window mount. Place this on the face of the other mount and press down well to ensure good adhesion.

Covering a mount (mat) with fabric adds richness and depth to a background, especially if you use a luxury fabric such as silk or velvet. Traditionally, Persian and Indian textiles were framed in a fabric mount.

Fabric-covered Mount

you will need
pre-cut mount (mat)
fabric
cutting mat
tape measure
craft knife
ruler
fabric glue
glue brush
ink roller

1 Place the pre-cut mount (mat) face down on the fabric, on a cutting mat. Cut out the fabric 2.5cm/1in larger all around to allow for overlaps. Trim the corners of the fabric to make folding over easier.

2 Apply a thin, even coat of fabric glue to the face of the mount. Centre the fabric on top of the mount, press down and rub gently with a clean ink roller to ensure good adhesion.

3 Turn over the covered mount so that the fabric is face down. Cut out the window, leaving a 2.5cm/1in border of fabric for the overlaps.

4 Cut mitres in the overlap fabric in the window. Apply fabric glue to the mount where the overlaps will lie, then fold over the fabric edges and press down firmly.

5 Fold down the overlaps on the side edges of the mount. At the corners, hold the fabric firmly and cut a mitre with a craft knife, then apply fabric glue and press the fabric down.

Mounts (mats) with a curved edge can be cut using a special bevel mount cutter. The curve can be cut freehand following a line or around a template in the shape and size required.

Shaped Mounts

Round mount

It is possible to cut around a saucer or plate to make a circular window, although this method limits the size of the frame you can use.

you will need
mount (mat) board cut to fit frame
2 pieces of scrap mount board
ruler
pencil
template
bevel mount (mat) cutter
map pins
straight edge

Below: Shaped mounts look effective around small subjects such as portrait miniatures or studies of single flowers.

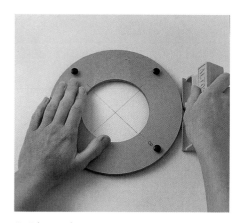

1 Place the mount (mat) board right side up on top of two pieces of scrap board to protect the work surface. Position a ruler diagonally across the corners and mark the centre. Pin the template to the board centred on the pencil mark.

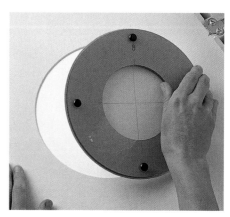

2 Place the cutter next to the template. Push the cutter forward and down until the blade is in the mount board and the bottom of the cutter is flat. Cut a quarter of the way around the template, keeping the contact points on the cutter flush with the template and the cutter flat.

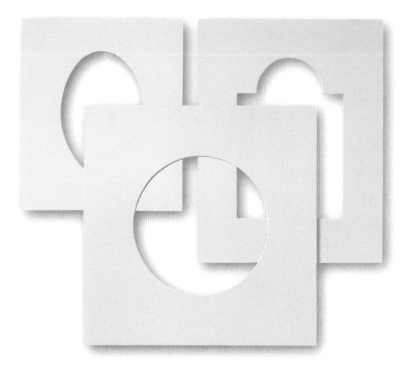

3 Leave the cutter in place and rotate the three layers of board a quarter-turn. Cut another quarter and rotate again. Repeat all the way around. Lift out the template and window.

Combination mount

This interesting shape resembles an arched window and is made using a round template at the top of a rectangular opening.

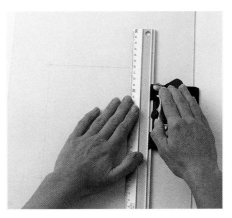

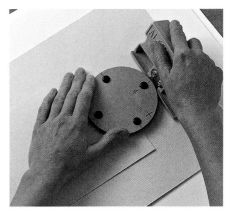

1 Measure the picture horizontally and vertically. Add 6cm/2¼in to the sides and the top, and 6.5cm/2½ in to the bottom. Following these measurements, cut the mount (mat) board to size and draw the shape on the reverse side. Tuck two pieces of scrap mount board underneath.

2 Line up the straight edge on the outside of the marked line. Push the mount cutter into the board just beyond the crossover point and move steadily along the line to just beyond the crossover point at the other end. Cut the remaining sides.

3 Turn the mount over and fit the window scrap back in position. Mark the centre point of the circle template on the right side and pin in position. Cut around the template.

Oval mount

An oval template can be drawn and, with practice, cut freehand. This method makes an oval to an exact width and height.

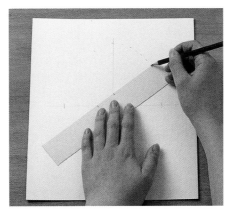

3 Mark the board then move the strip about 9mm/⅜in round, keeping the centre marks on the horizontal and vertical lines, and mark the board again. Keep moving the strip round until the first quarter is complete. Repeat to complete each quarter in turn until the oval is finished.

1 Determine the size of oval required. Divide the mount (mat) board vertically and horizontally with two pencil lines at right angles to each other. Mark the length and width of the oval on the lines.

2 Place a strip of thin cardboard on the horizontal line and mark the centre and width of the oval. Turn the strip vertically and place the width point on the height point. Mark the new centre position on the strip. Place the strip across the two axes near the vertical, aligning the two centre marks with the two axis lines.

4 Tuck a couple of pieces of scrap mount board under the marked oval. Insert map pins inside the oval to secure the layers. Use a mount cutter freehand to cut along the line. Leave the cutter in the mount board and turn the boards as you cut each quarter, taking care to join the two ends of the cut neatly.

Window mounts (mats) can be decorated in lots of different ways. Decorative papers, ruled lines, washes and marbling add extra richness around the aperture and will complement and enhance the picture.

Decorating a Mount

Marbled border

you will need
pre-cut mount (mat)
soft pencil
ruler or straight edge
decorative paper
cutting mat
craft knife
spray adhesive or PVA (white) glue

The subtle colour combinations of marbled or other decorated paper make a pretty border for a delicate sketch or painting.

1 On the face of the pre-cut mount (mat), mark out light lines with a pencil and ruler or straight edge, setting out where the decorative border is to be placed. Place the decorative paper on a cutting mat to protect the surface. Using a craft knife and ruler, measure and cut the paper into appropriate-sized strips.

2 Spray adhesive on the reverse of the strips and stick them along the lines.

3 Using a ruler and craft knife, mitre each corner. Remove the spare paper.

Decorative lines

Lines are normally drawn in gold or a soft shade such as grey or sepia. Single lines are usually drawn between 5–15mm/¼–⅝in away from the bevel. Double lines usually have a 3–5mm/⅛–¼in gap between them.

you will need

corner gauge

pencil

pre-cut mount (mat)

lining ink

distilled water

lining pen

scrap mount (mat) board

small watercolour brush

bevelled ruler

eraser

1 Use a corner gauge to mark the position of the lines lightly on the mount (mat) with a sharp pencil. Dilute the lining ink to the required shade with distilled water (tap water can leave brown marks as it dries). Test the colour on a piece of scrap board.

2 Adjust the prongs of the lining pen to the required width. Load the pen with ink using a small watercolour brush. You need enough to complete the line but not so much that the ink comes out in a blob.

3 Draw the line between the dots using a ruler with a bevel edge to prevent the ink bleeding. Turn the mount round and draw the remaining lines. Once the ink has dried, the pencil marks can be erased without damaging the lines.

Colourwashing

Watercolour paint can be diluted with distilled water to create a very pale wash.

To add more colour around a mount (mat), paint in a light wash between two ink lines. Use a brush that is the exact width of the gap. Mix distilled water with watercolour paint to make a very pale wash. Paint on a wash of clear water first to delay the drying process, then brush the colour between the lines.

Below: A selection of decorative effects to enhance the artwork displayed.

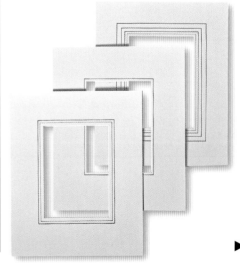

▶

Sponging

Sponging is a quick and easy way to decorate a mount (mat). Use a combination of pale colours that blend well together, then outline them with a fine line to provide definition.

you will need

pencil

corner gauge

pre-cut mount (mat)

magic tape

ruler

craft knife

acrylic paint

palette or plate

natural sponge

paper towels

lining ink

lining pen

bevelled ruler

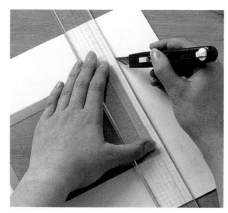

1 Using a sharp pencil and corner gauge, mark the position of the lines and area to be sponged on the mount (mat). Stick lengths of magic tape outside the marks on the corners of the mount to blank off the area to be decorated. Using a ruler and craft knife, cut the tape flush at the corners.

2 Mix the paint colours required. Dip the sponge in the first colour and remove the excess on a paper towel. Gently dab the sponge between the pieces of magic tape.

3 Wash the sponge and dry it by squeezing it out in a paper towel. Apply a second colour with the sponge to achieve the desired effect. Allow the paint to dry and then carefully peel off the magic tape.

4 Draw lines in a toning colour on each side of the sponging. To avoid smudging the ink, draw all the inside lines first, turning the mount around for each line, and then complete the outside lines.

Successful framing is all about choosing a mount (mat) and frame that suits the image and takes into account where it will hang. A successful result occurs when the combination of colour, texture, size and shape is balanced.

Choosing Mount Sizes

◄▲ The frames left and above demonstrate how the same image can look completely different when treated in two different ways. A very small image may look lost on a wall if it is displayed individually in a small frame. The large frame pictured on the left has a large expanse of mount (mat) board. It draws the eye into the image in the centre of the frame. This image demands to be looked at. The style shown above would work well as part of a group of similar frames.

◄ Mount pairs or groups of small images together in one frame to increase the picture area. Choose the shape of the picture to suit the position where it will hang. Long rectangular pictures, for instance, can be used to fill the wall space between two windows or doors.

Two methods of securing the artwork to the backing board are shown here. Book mounts are for squared-up images where the picture edges are hidden. A float mount is for images whose edges are on display.

Securing the Artwork

Book mount   Paper tapes at the upper edge of the artwork hold it in place, while the mount (mat) and backing board are simply hinged together at the top.

you will need
pre-cut window mount (mat)
artwork
backing board
acid-free hinging tape
self-adhesive fabric tape

1 Make the window at least 5mm/¼in smaller than the image.

2 Stick two short pieces of acid-free tape to the underside of the image.

3 Stick a second piece across the free end of each length of tape to make two tab hinges. There should be a gap between the top of the picture and the second pieces of tape. Leave the tape to dry.

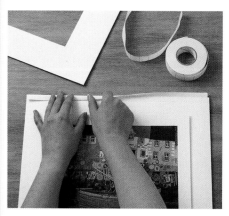

4 Stick a length of self-adhesive fabric tape along the top edge of the backing board so that half of the tape is above the edge. Fold the tape back on itself and crease with the edge of your thumbnail. Position the mount on top and press in place.

Float mount

you will need

pre-cut window mount (mat) (reserving
cut-out section of board)
backing board
artwork
acid-free hinging tape
craft knife
ruler
self-healing cutting mat
self-adhesive fabric tape

This invisible method of mounting is for artwork that is smaller than the aperture. Images printed on handmade paper that has an attractive deckle edge are often mounted in this way.

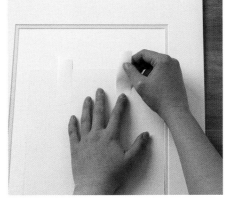

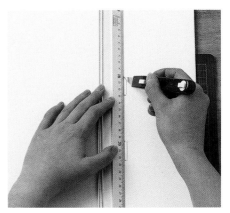

1 Place the mount (mat) on top of the backing board and position the artwork face down in the window. Tear two 5cm/2in strips of hinging tape, dampen the last 5mm/¼in of each and stick to the artwork approximately 2.5cm/1in from the top.

2 Mark the positions of the paper hinges on the backing board. Using a craft knife and working on a cutting mat, cut two 5mm/¼in slots through the backing board at the marked positions. Cut the slots wide enough to feed the hinges through.

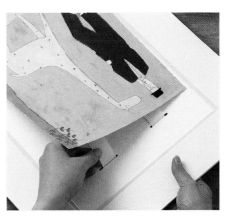

3 Attach the backing board to the window mount as for the book mount opposite. Place the artwork in position and feed the tapes through the slots. Make sure the artwork is in exactly the right position in the mount. Fit the cut-out section from the mount back in the aperture to hold the artwork in position and turn the mount over. Dampen the free ends of the pieces of tape and stick them to the back of the backing board to secure the artwork.

Mouldings are the decoratively shaped lengths of wood used to make up the frame. They are available in a variety of finishes and are always described by their profile – that is, their cross-sections or end-views.

Mouldings

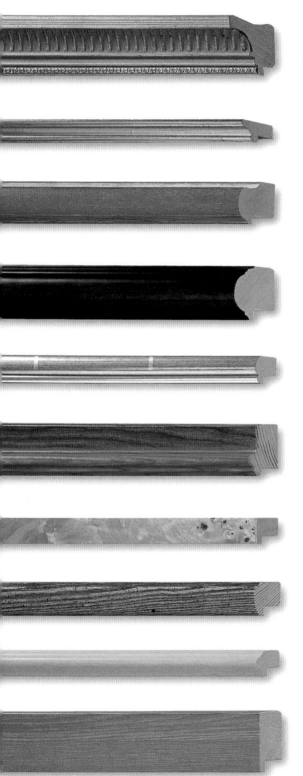

Mouldings are usually sold in 1.8m/6ft or 2.4m/8ft lengths and are available from builders' merchants, timber yards, art suppliers or framers.

There are two basic types of moulding: picture frame moulding and builders' moulding. The main difference between the two is that picture frame moulding includes a pre-cut rebate, a step that accommodates the artwork, mount (mat), glass and backing board and stops them collapsing through the front of the frame.

Builders' moulding is fundamentally intended for trimming internal structures such as door frames, windows and skirting boards, and consequently does not need to incorporate a rebate. To convert builders' moulding it is necessary to create a suitable recess by attaching narrow strips of wood, called fillets, under the moulding before assembling the frame.

Manufactured moulding is often pre-decorated and finished. Many styles are available, from reproduction, antiqued, metal and highly decorated, to plain wood. Natural wood mouldings leave the embellishment in the hands of the framer. Ash and oak have a pleasing grain, and lime-waxing or woodstaining enhances it. Obeche and ramin are woods that are suitable for more opaque or solid decoration. One factor to take into consideration is whether the wood is a softwood or a hardwood. For example, ash and oak are very hard and take some perseverance to cut, whereas obeche, pine and ramin are fairly easy to cut.

▼

Multiple lengths of moulding make a dramatic deep frame for a tiny image.

▼

This modern gilded frame sets off the golden leaves in the picture.

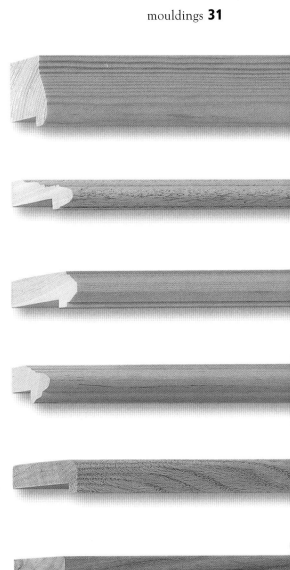

▲

Use a subtle bamboo-effect moulding, to enhance an image with an Oriental theme. The width of the frame also mirrors the width of the leaves and adds a delicacy to this large picture.

▲

A small but powerful image stands out well in an opulent frame.

▶

A slim moulding looks elegant around a small image in a large mount (mat).

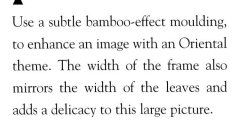

▼

This colourwashed moulding has a ripple effect that echoes the waves on the sea. Its rough wood finish looks a little like driftwood and the bold colour suits the naive image perfectly.

There are several ways of cutting a length of moulding to make a basic frame, but the ends must always be cut at a precise angle. You can use either a mitre clamp or a wooden mitre box to guide the saw.

Cutting and Joining a Basic Frame

you will need

tape measure

moulding

mitre clamp or box

saw

pencil

PVA (white) glue and brush

frame clamp

cloth

V-nail joiner and V-nails or vice,

panel pins (brads) and tack hammer

woodfiller

cork sanding block

medium- and fine-grade sandpaper

(glasspaper)

1 Measure the mounted artwork to give you the inside rebate measurement for the frame. Hold the length of moulding in a mitre clamp or box and cut the first end at a 45° angle. The edge of the moulding with the rebate should be the furthest from you.

2 Measure along the inside rebate of the moulding and mark the position for the next mitre cut on the face of the moulding.

3 Insert the moulding in the mitre clamp or box and saw at a 45° angle along the marked line.

4 Place the moulding in the mitre clamp or box. To make the next section of the frame, cut away the triangular "offcut" as in step 1 with the same 45° angle. Do this before you measure the second cut.

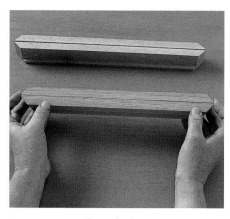

5 Measure and mark the second cut on the moulding. Repeat the steps until all four lengths are cut. Check that each pair – the two side lengths and the lengths for the top and bottom – is an exact match.

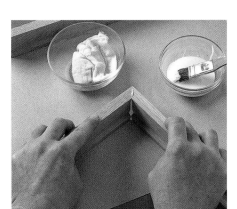

6 Using PVA (white) glue, secure two sections of the moulding together to make a right angle. Repeat with the other sections, then join them all together to make the frame.

9 Turn the frame right side up and fill the mitred corners with woodfiller. Wipe away any excess woodfiller with a damp cloth. Allow to dry.

10 Use a cork block and medium-grade sandpaper (glasspaper) to sand all over the frame and the rebate. Repeat with finer-grade sandpaper.

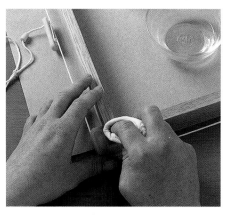

7 Secure the frame clamp around the frame to hold the glued pieces together. Wipe away any excess glue with a damp cloth before it begins to set, otherwise it will form a waterproof barrier sealing the wood and any colourwash or woodstain you choose to use will not stain the wood around the joints.

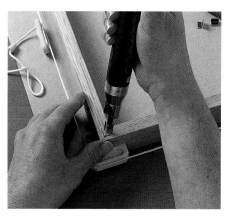

8 Turn the frame right side down and insert V-nails into the corners of the back of the frame using a hand-held underpinner tool. Or, place the right-angled corners of the frame in a vice, and hammer panel pins (brads) into the corner edges of the moulding using a tack hammer. Once all four corners have been pinned, leave to dry.

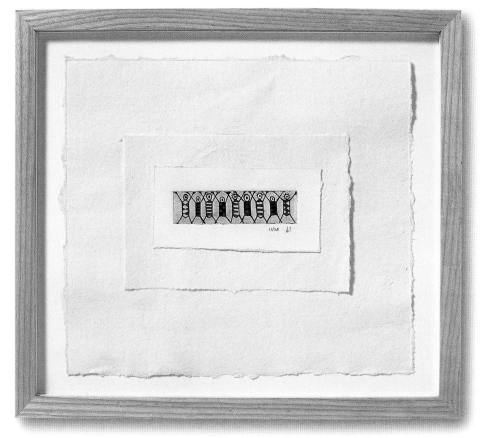

Builder's architrave, used for skirting boards and door frames, can be used to make sturdy inexpensive frames. Architrave is flat on the reverse, so to enable it to hold a picture, glass and backing board you need to create a rebate.

Creating a Rebate

Using a router

you will need

power router

rebate cutter with ball-bearing pilot tip

spanner (US wrench)

2 G-clamps

2 lengths of architrave

A power router is quick to set up and the finished results are very professional. Edge-forming cutters have a rotating tip that runs along the edge of the wood. The rebate can be cut on lengths of moulding before making up the frame, or on the finished frame.

1 Select a rebate cutter with a ball-bearing pilot tip. An edge-forming pilot tip allows the router to run along the edge of the architrave without a guide rail. Ensure the router is switched off, loosen the collet nut and fit the rebate cutter. Tighten the collet nut with a spanner.

2 Clamp the length of architrave face down on a workbench. Clamp a second length in front of it on which to balance the router. Adjust the depth scale on the side of the router to the exact depth of the rebate required.

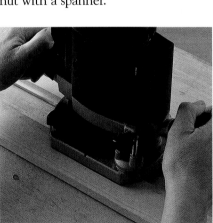

◀ **3** Balance the router on the two pieces of wood. Switch it on and use the plunge mechanism to drop the router on to the depth stop. Tighten the plunge-lock handle. Holding the router with both hands, advance the router into the architrave, using light pressure to move it along the length of the wood. Release the plunging mechanism when you reach the end and switch off.

Using fillets

Create a rebate by fitting lengths of wood, called fillets, on the reverse side of the frame. The depth of the wood should be the same as the required rebate – usually 1cm/½in. The width of the wood must be at least 5mm/¼in narrower than the architrave, but if you do not want to see the fillet at the outer edge of the frame the width should be narrower still.

1 Measure the artwork to determine the inside measurement of the frame. Cut the first end of the architrave with a mitre saw set at 45°. Measure the length required on the inside edge of the architrave. Turn the saw to the other side and line it up against the mark. Cut the second end. Cut two pieces of architrave for the sides and two for the top and bottom of the frame. Spread the cut ends with glue and assemble the frame.

2 Fit a frame clamp on each corner and tighten the cord. Leave the glue to dry thoroughly.

3 Turn the frame over. Put a V-nail on the magnetic tip of the V-nail joiner with the sharp edge up. Check that the V-nail is correctly positioned across the joint and push down firmly. Repeat at each corner of the frame. You may need to use a mallet to drive the nails into harder woods.

4 Cut the fillet at 45° at one end. Add 1cm/½in to the inside length measurement of the frame, to allow for the rebate, and mark the fillet. Turn the saw to the other side. Line it up with the mark and cut the other end. Cut four pieces of fillet – one for each side of the frame.

5 Spread glue on the underside of the fillet pieces and arrange on the reverse side of the architrave frame. Butt the mitred corners together so that the rebate is the same depth all the way around. Hammer a panel pin (brad) through the fillet and into the architrave every 5cm/2in along each length and leave to dry.

Combine two or three picture-framing mouldings to make your own made-to-measure frame. Two treatments are given to the mouldings chosen for this project: black stain, and a natural polyurethane varnish.

Using Decorative Mouldings

you will need

tenon saw

wood glue

mitre block

Black Frame

1.6m/64in barley twist moulding

80cm/32in semicircular moulding

80cm/32in flat moulding

black woodstain or ink

paintbrush

black shoe polish

soft cloth

shoe brush

Natural Frame

80cm/32in of 5mm/¼in square moulding

80cm/32in of 1.5 × 2cm/⅝in × ¾in flat moulding

2.4m/2⅝yd decorative moulding

corner clamps

clear polyurethane varnish and brush

Black Frame

1 Using a tenon saw, cut 20cm/8in lengths from each piece of moulding. Using wood glue, join a barley twist and a semi-circular moulding strip to each side of the flat moulding. (The semicircular moulding will form the rebate of the frame.) Allow the glue to dry completely.

2 Mitre the lengths of assembled moulding using a mitre block and tenon saw, and make up the frame (see Pressed Flowerhead Frame steps 1–4). Mitre the remaining barley twist moulding and glue around the centre front of the frame. Allow to dry.

3 Stain the frame with black ink or woodstain applied with a paintbrush.

4 When the stain is dry, seal the wood and add a sheen with black shoe polish, applied with a soft cloth. Buff it up with a shoe brush.

Natural Frame

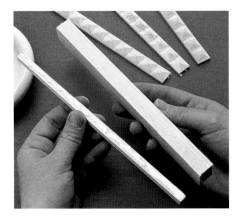

1 Using a tenon saw, cut four 20cm/8in lengths of square moulding. Cut four pieces of flat moulding to the same length. Glue a piece of square moulding to one edge of each piece of flat moulding.

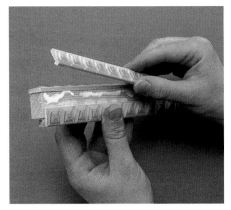

2 Cut 12 pieces of decorative moulding, each 20cm/8in long. Glue two decorative mouldings to the front surface and one on the side. Leave the glue to dry thoroughly.

3 Mitre the ends of the assembled pieces, using a mitre block and tenon saw. Glue and clamp the corners accurately together.

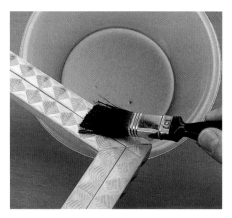

4 Apply one or more coats of clear polyurethane varnish to seal the wood and enhance the natural colours and grain of the wood.

You can use a mitre saw to make frames with more than four corners. To make a hexagonal frame the moulding is cut at an angle of 60°. The blade angle is usually indicated on the clamp, making the cutting process foolproof.

Hexagonal Frame

you will need

mitre clamp

saw

moulding

pencil (optional)

craft knife

wood glue and glue brush

frame clamp

V-nails

V-nail joiner

hammer (optional)

wax

cloth

1 Clamp the mitre saw to the work surface so that you get a smooth cutting action. Move the blade to the 60° mark on the mitre saw. Place the moulding under the saw so that the end juts out beyond the blade. Clamp it in place and cut the first angle.

2 Loosen the clamp and move the moulding along to the required length. Mark the length with a pencil or use the ruler on the mitre clamp. Turn the saw to 60° on the opposite side and cut the moulding.

3 Turn the saw back to the other side. Move the moulding along so that it juts out beyond the blade again ready to cut the second piece. Repeat the steps above to cut six identical pieces.

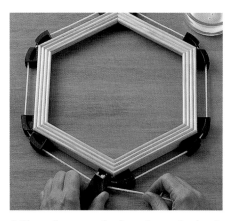

4 Trim the saw whiskers from the back of each piece of moulding with a craft knife. Spread a little wood glue on both ends of each piece. Arrange and join the pieces on a flat surface and clamp with a frame clamp. Leave the glue to dry overnight.

5 Turn the frame over to the reverse side. Push two V-nails into each joint with a V-nail joiner. If the wood is too hard, tap the end of the tool with a hammer. Remove the frame clamp and polish the frame with wax.

Right: For an octagonal frame set the angle of the mitre saw to 45 degrees.

Instead of making a mitre at each corner, this design for a sturdy frame employs halving joints, cut using a saw and chisel. Halving joints rely on glue for their strength but can be reinforced with dowels or screws.

Halving Joint Frame

you will need

tape measure

pencil

12 x 50mm/½ x 2in wood

tenon saw

T-square

bench hook

clamp

chisel and mallet

wood glue and glue brush

5mm/¼in dowel

drill and 5mm/¼in drill bit

tack hammer

medium- and fine-grade sandpaper

(glasspaper)

1 Measure the artwork horizontally and vertically to determine the aperture size of the frame. Add twice the width of the wood to each measurement to find the length and width of the frame. Cut two pieces of wood the length and two the width of the frame.

2 Use one of the cut pieces to mark the width of the wood at both ends of each piece. Use the square to mark the wood across the width and down the side. Mark the centre line on both sides at each end of the wood.

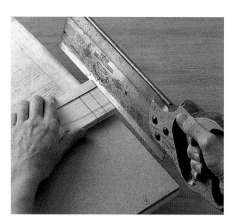

3 Fit the marked wood against a bench hook and saw along the line through to the halfway mark, bringing the saw to the horizontal to make a straight cut. Make two or three further saw cuts to make chiselling out the waste easier.

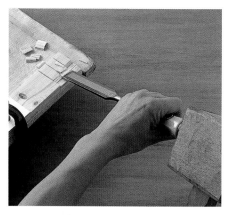

4 Secure the wood to the bench with a clamp. Using the chisel and a mallet cut away the waste wood above the line. Turn the wood round and chisel out from the other side.

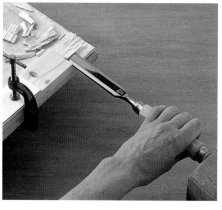

5 Once most of the wood is removed, work with the chisel horizontally to remove the remaining raised portion in the middle. Cut all four frame pieces in the same way with the cut joints on the same side.

6 Turn the side sections over to the reverse side and assemble the frame. Glue the cut surfaces of the joints and clamp together. Check the corners are square and leave to dry.

7 For a stronger, more decorative dowelled joint, mark a diagonal line from the corner of the aperture to the outer corner of the frame. Measure along this line to mark the dowel positions. Cut eight pieces of dowel the same depth as the frame.

8 Clamp the frame to scrap wood and drill through at each mark. Drop a little glue into each hole. Tap the pieces of dowel into the holes and leave to dry. Sand the edges of the joints so that they are flush with the frame.

you will need
wooden frame
4 decorative frame corners
PVA (white) glue and brush
acrylic paint
paintbrush
varnish or wax

Adding decorative corners

To give a plain frame a more individual appearance, add decorative corners and paint them to match the frame. Corners are available in a variety of styles and sizes and are sold by most art and picture framing suppliers.

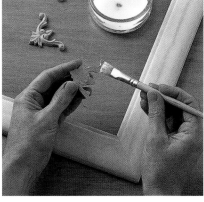

1 Apply glue to the reverse of each frame corner in turn, then position them at each corner of the frame. Leave to dry on a flat surface.

2 Cover the frame, including the corners, with two coats of acrylic paint and leave to dry. Varnish or wax the frame as required.

The traditional cross-over frame, often known as a school frame, is quite easy to make. The skill is in making each joint exactly the right size so that the sides of the frame fit securely together.

Cross-over Frame

you will need

tape measure

length of square section wood, 15mm/⅝ in wide

pencil

tenon saw

bench hook or vice

G-clamp

chisel

flat surform file

coarse sandpaper (glasspaper)

fine sanding pad

PVA (white) glue and brush

board and weight

rubber (latex) gloves

soft cloths

dark woodstain

black patinating wax

1 Measure the artwork and mount (mat) board horizontally and vertically to find the aperture size of the frame. Add 9cm/3½ in to each measurement to determine the lengths of wood required for the frame. Cut two lengths and two widths.

2 Mark the wood 9cm/3½ in from each end. Use a spare piece of the wood to mark the width of the joint and square the lines. Mark the halfway line on each side of the wood. Fit the wood in a bench hook or vice. Saw just inside each line down to the halfway mark. Turn the wood around and cut the other end in the same way. Cut all four pieces.

3 Clamp the wood to the bench and chisel out the waste wood a little at a time. On narrow wood strips use the chisel vertically with the flat surface towards the marked line. Push down firmly to remove the wood bit by bit.

4 To shape the edges of the frame, hold a flat surform file at an angle across the edge of the wood. File the wood between the chiselled-out sections until there is a 3–5mm/⅛–¼ in flat surface that tapers off at each end.

5 Shape the ends of each piece using the surform. This time the shaped edge is tapered near the cut-out section and then comes right off the end rather than tapering again. Shape the ends of each piece.

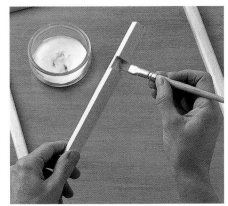

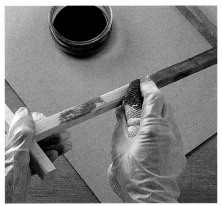

6 Sand all the shaped edges with coarse sandpaper (glasspaper) until they are smooth and rounded. Finish off with a fine sanding pad.

7 To assemble the frame, arrange the top and bottom sections of the frame the correct distance apart. Spread glue on all the sides of the cut-out sections of one of the side pieces and fit in place. Glue the other side in place. Place a board and weight on top of the frame until the glue dries.

8 Using a soft cloth, wipe the wood with a dark woodstain, making sure there is no bare wood showing in any inside corners around the cross-over joints. Leave to dry. To finish the frame, rub black patinating wax into the wood and buff up the surface with a clean cloth.

Any shape of frame can be cut from medium density fibreboard using a carpenter's jigsaw. Draw your design and simply cut around it. You can cut the rebate into the aperture using a router.

Jigsaw Puzzle Frame

you will need

pencil

cardboard

craft knife

cutting mat

medium-density fibreboard (MDF), 9mm/⅜in thick

marker pen

2 G-clamps

protective face mask

jigsaw with 2mm/¹⁄₁₆in blade suitable for MDF

ruler

piece of scrap wood

drill and 8mm/⅜in bit

medium-grade sandpaper (glasspaper)

fine sanding pad

router with rebate cutter

cloth

acrylic paint

paintbrush

backing board

panel pins (brads)

tack hammer

1 Draw a jigsaw puzzle shape template on cardboard and cut it out using a craft knife and working on a cutting mat. Place the template on the medium density fibreboard (MDF) and draw around it using a marker pen. Clamp the MDF to the workbench so that the line you are going to cut first is clear of the bench. Wear a protective face mask when working with MDF to avoid inhaling dust particles.

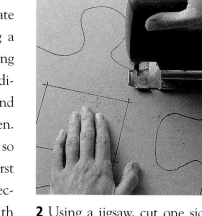

2 Using a jigsaw, cut one side of the frame just outside the drawn line. Turn the template around to the next side. Continue turning and cutting until all four sides are cut.

3 In each corner of the aperture, draw an 8mm/⁵⁄₁₆in square using a pencil and ruler and mark across each square on the diagonal to find its centre.

4 Place the frame on a piece of scrap wood and clamp in position. Drill through the MDF into the scrap wood at each centre point. Secure the frame to the workbench so that the first side of the aperture is clear of the work surface. Cut along the line between the two holes. Turn the frame around and cut the other sides in turn.

5 Sand the frame edges. If you are making frames to link together, check the fit. Adjust as necessary. Finish the frame with a fine sanding pad.

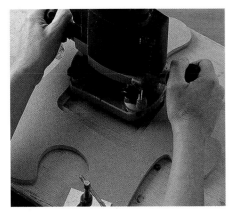

6 Fit a rebate cutter into the router. Clamp the frame face down on the workbench. Set the router depth. Place the router in the aperture. Cut out the rebate, then sand the frame. Wipe the surface with a damp cloth.

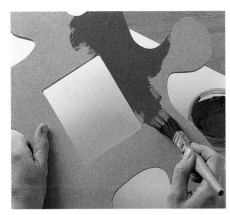

7 Paint the frame as desired. Cut a backing board to fit the aperture. Insert the picture, then the backing, and secure with panel pins (brads).

Similar in effect to a multi-window mount (mat), this frame is ideal for collections of objects – in this case, pressed leaves – and creates a dramatic three-dimensional effect. Finish the surface with Danish oil.

Multi-window Frame

1 With a tape measure, T-square and pencil, mark the lengths and widths of the plywood and saw the pieces to size. Butt the plywood pieces together to check that they fit. Cut the back of the frame and set aside. Sand down all the edges.

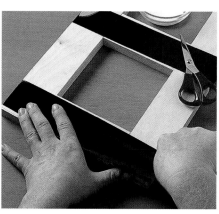

2 Apply PVA (white) glue to the ends of the horizontals and assemble the frame. Wrap self-adhesive sealing tape around the frame, both front and back. Wipe off the excess glue at once with a damp cloth and leave overnight to dry.

3 Once the glue has set, remove the tape. Use medium-grade sandpaper (glasspaper) with a cork sanding block to sand the face and all edges of the frame. For a smooth finish, sand again with fine-grade sandpaper.

4 Place some Danish wood oil in a dish. Wearing rubber (latex) gloves, apply the oil over the wood in a circular motion using a soft cloth. Work the oil into the wood. Buff up with a clean soft cloth.

5 Apply a line of glue to the front of the backing board, approximately 3cm/1¼ in in from the edge. Stick the fabric on to it. Leave to dry.

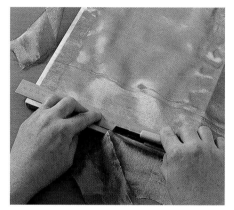

6 Trim the excess fabric using a metal ruler and craft knife.

7 Apply glue to the back of the frame front, then align the frame front and backing board and stick the two halves together.

8 Place heavy weights or G-clamps on each corner and the middle section of the frame. Place a cloth below the weights or clamps to prevent damage to the face of the frame. Wipe away excess glue with a damp cloth and leave to dry overnight.

9 Apply a coat of oil to the side edges of the backing board. Find the centre of each window and hammer in a large-headed nail, leaving approximately 1cm/½ in showing. Mix a small amount of epoxy resin glue and apply this to the nail heads. Place a leaf on each nail and leave to set.

Good, clean driftwood can be hard to find even if you live near the sea, but you can make your own "driftwood" from old boards or packing crates. Break up the wood and distress the lengths with a chisel.

Driftwood Frame

you will need

packing crate or wooden board

chisel

hammer

surform file

coarse-grade sandpaper (glasspaper)

watercolour paints: green, crimson and blue

paintbrushes

epoxy resin glue

coping saw

hardboard

chalkboard paint

masking tape

drill

sisal string, 1m/1⅛yd

scissors

thick sisal rope, 1m/1⅛yd

1 Split the wood into narrower lengths using a chisel and a hammer.

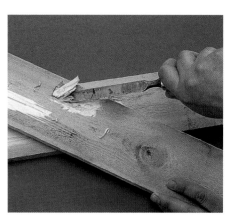

2 Select four suitable lengths of similar width for the sides of the frame. Gouge chunks from the sides of the wood to make it look weatherbeaten.

4 Sand the wood down with coarse-grade sandpaper (glasspaper) to remove any splinters, and round off the edges.

5 Mix a thin colourwash using green, crimson and blue watercolour paints and brush it on to the wood. Allow the wood to dry.

3 Use a surform to file away the edges of the wood until they are smooth.

6 Glue the frame together with epoxy resin glue and allow to dry. Cut a piece of hardboard to fit the back of the frame and paint the smooth side with chalkboard paint.

7 Tape the chalkboard to the back of the frame. Drill a hole in each corner through all the layers. Thread each end of a length of sisal string through the holes at the bottom of the frame, working from the back to the front. Knot the ends on the front of the frame. Trim any excess string.

8 Enlarge the two holes at the top of the frame and pass thick sisal rope through the holes as before, leaving enough excess rope to hang the frame. Tie a knot in each end on the front of the frame.

Reclaimed timber has a natural distressed and heavy appearance. This frame requires no finish, relying instead on its natural characteristics for its rugged appeal.

Reclaimed Timber Frame

you will need

reclaimed timber:

2 verticals, 62 x 10cm/25 x 4in

2 horizontals, 18 x 10cm/7 x 4in

tape measure

pencil

tenon saw

sandpaper (glasspaper)

hardboard, 54 x 28cm/22 x 11in

coping saw

fabric glue and brush

black felt

decorative paper

PVA (white) glue and brush

chalk

bradawl (awl)

14 screws, 2.5cm/1in long

screwdriver

4 reclaimed brackets

8 galvanized nails, 2.5cm/1in long

hammer

fillets, 5mm/¼in deep

natural objects for framing

1 On the timber, measure and mark with a pencil the length and width of the frame verticals and horizontals. Use a tenon saw to cut the timber to the correct sizes. Lightly sand the sawn edges. Cut the hardboard backing board to size. Apply fabric glue to the back, then stick a piece of black felt on top. Glue decorative paper to the face of the backing board.

2 Mark out corner holes for the screws, using chalk. Turn the cut lengths of timber face down and butt them together at the corners. Place the felt-covered hardboard on the back of the timber. Make initial holes in the hardboard with a bradawl (awl), then screw into the back of the frame. The screws will hold the frame together.

3 Turn the frame the right way up and nail in the reclaimed brackets, using galvanized nails.

4 Cut small fillets to size, coat with PVA (white) glue, and use them to mount the framed objects to give a three-dimensional effect.

A deep-sided, sectioned frame is the perfect way to display a collection of small objects such as ornaments, jewellery or badges. Custom-build the sections to suit the size of the objects in your collection.

Box Frame

you will need
length of batten, 30 x 5mm/1¼ x ¼in
pencil
metal ruler
junior hacksaw
wood glue
panel pins (brads)
hammer
hardboard
jigsaw or coping saw
white acrylic primer
paintbrush
length of batten, 30 x 2mm/1¼ x ¹⁄₁₆in
masking tape
PVA (white) glue and brush
tissue paper in assorted colours
acrylic paint: yellow and blue
artist's brushes
small Indian shisha glass

1 Using the thicker battening, measure and cut four sides of the rectangular frame, then glue them together with wood glue and secure with panel pins (brads).

2 Cut a piece of hardboard to fit the frame and paint the smooth front side with acrylic primer. When dry, glue and pin it to the back of the frame.

3 Measure and draw out all the compartments. Cut the dividers from the length of thinner battening.

4 Assemble the compartments inside the box frame with wood glue, taping them in position with masking tape until the glue has set.

5 Coat the inside of each compartment with PVA (white) glue and cover with pieces of torn tissue paper. Work the tissue paper into the corners and keep applying the glue. Use light colours over strong colours to create depth.

6 Carefully retouch any areas of the compartments that need more colour, using yellow acrylic paint. Allow the paint to dry.

7 Use wood glue to attach lengths of the thinner battening to the outer edge of the frame, in effect creating a rebate. Leave the glue to dry.

8 Cover the edge of the frame with a collage of blue tissue paper, using PVA glue.

9 Using an artist's brush, lightly brush over the tissue paper with blue acrylic paint. Leave to dry.

10 Glue small Indian shisha glass all around the frame. Arrange your collection in the compartments, securing the pieces with glue.

In this type of frame, the artwork sits flush with the face of the frame. A gap is left around the edge of the canvas to give it depth. Here the frame is colourwashed to match the colours in the painting.

Framing a Canvas

you will need
tape measure
painted, stretched canvas
pencil
wooden frame, prepared and sanded
gouache paint: ultramarine and black
paintbrush
bowl
cloth
batten, 2.5cm/1in wide, 5mm/¼in deep
tenon saw
hardboard
jigsaw or coping saw
emulsion (latex) paint: black
PVA (white) glue and brush
framer's point gun
panel pins (brads) and tack hammer
(optional)
bradawl (awl)
screws, 1cm/½in long
screwdriver
self-adhesive backing tape
craft knife

1 Measure the canvas and add on 1cm/½in to the vertical and horizontal measurements. This will give a 5mm/¼in gap around the canvas when it is eventually inserted into the frame. Measure the depth of the canvas and choose a frame that is deep enough to allow the canvas to lie flush with the face of the frame.

2 Mix two parts ultramarine gouache with one part black gouache in a bowl. Blend together and add four parts water. Mix well with a paintbrush. This is a very opaque colourwash solution. Apply the wash in long, smooth strokes on the face and then the side edges of the frame. Leave to dry.

3 Place the frame face down on a piece of cloth. Measure the inside vertical and horizontal edges of the frame. These measurements are for the fillets and the backing board. Mark and saw the fillets and the hardboard to fit inside the rebate.

4 Using black emulsion (latex) paint, paint one face and edge of all the fillets and a strip approximately 5cm/2in wide around the edge of the face of the hardboard. Leave to dry. Neatly paint the edge of the canvas.

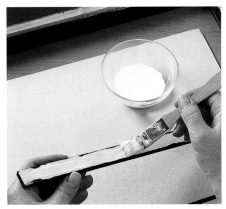

5 Once the fillets have dried, apply PVA (white) glue to the unpainted side of each one and place them around the sides of the frame.

6 When the fillets are secure, place the backing board, painted side facing inwards, in the frame and pin in position, using a framer's point gun. Alternatively use panel pins (brads) and a tack hammer.

7 Place the canvas in the frame and hold it in place. On the back make a hole aligning with each corner of the canvas using a bradawl (awl). Screw the hardboard to the canvas. Tape up the back of the frame.

If the image you are going to frame is simple and plain, you can add decorative interest by insetting objects into the frame. Choose a wide moulding with enough depth to allow shapes to be chiselled out.

Insetting Objects into a Frame

you will need

wooden frame, prepared and sanded
metal ruler
soft pencil
craft knife
chisel and hammer
medium- and fine-grade sandpaper
(glasspaper)
cork sanding block
soft cloth
rubber (latex) gloves
oil paint: olive green
black cardboard
cutting mat
PVA (white) glue and glue brush
glass, 2mm/$\frac{1}{16}$in thick
glass cutter
T-square
Dutch metal leaf
glass etching spray
protective face mask
masking tape
slate pebbles and other decorative
objects
epoxy resin glue

1 Mark out oblongs and squares on the face of the frame with a ruler and soft pencil. Centre the shapes between the rebate and outside edge.

2 Score the pencil marks on the frame using a craft knife and a metal ruler. Chisel out the shapes quite deeply, so that the glass will not protrude from the face of the frame.

3 Sand the frame with medium-grade sandpaper (glasspaper) and a cork sanding block, then with a finer grade of sandpaper.

4 Using a soft cloth and wearing rubber (latex) gloves, apply olive green oil paint over the frame. Cut pieces of black cardboard for the background of each inset, and glue in place in the chiselled-out spaces.

5 Cut the glass for all the inserts to the sizes required using a glass cutter and a T-square. Decorate the underside of some pieces of the insert glass with Dutch metal leaf for an opaque effect. Spray a few of the glass pieces with a little glass etching spray, ensuring that the objects underneath will remain visible. Wear a protective face mask and work in a ventilated area.

6 Select the objects to be inserted in the inset panels. To decorate the glass for the slate pebbles, place masking tape in two strips over the glass and spray on the etching spray in a line down the centre, holding the can about 20cm/8in away. When the spray is dry, remove the tape to reveal a neat line of mottled glass.

7 Mark and cut out cardboard fillets to the appropriate size. Glue the fillets into the chiselled oblongs.

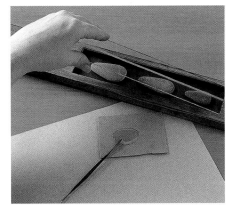

8 Glue the slate pebbles on to the black cardboard background using epoxy resin. Glue the glass on to the fillets using epoxy resin.

9 Add other decorative elements to the frame as desired. If the objects are flat, attach them to the glass with PVA glue, which will dry transparent.

Birch plywood is used in this unusual frame because of its strength. The heavier the stone you wish to frame, the thicker the plywood needs to be. For a heavy stone, replace the galvanized nails with strong screws.

Framing an Engraved Stone

you will need

tape measure

birch plywood, 18mm/¾in thick

tenon saw

drill and masonry bit

medium- and fine-grade sandpaper (glasspaper)

cork sanding block

rubber (latex) gloves

oil paint: olive green

soft cloths

galvanized nails, 2.5cm/1in long

tack hammer

1 Measure and saw the birch plywood to fit the stone plaque, allowing for a border of approximately 4cm/1½in all round. Using a drill with a masonry bit, drill four holes in the stone, one in each of the corners.

2 Sand the plywood, first with medium-, then fine-grade sandpaper (glasspaper), using a cork sanding block to smooth it down. Wearing rubber (latex) gloves, apply olive green oil paint with a soft cloth all over the plywood. Rub it well into the grain and buff with a clean, soft cloth.

3 Place the stone on the plywood and level up. Place a cloth over the galvanized nails to avoid marking the stone when you hammer them in through the drilled holes.

The decoration on this wide, flat frame uses a wonderfully simple technique to achieve the look of hand lettering. Photocopies of lettering, or even pictures, may be used in the same way.

Decorative Lettering

you will need

wooden frame, prepared and sanded

computer-generated text

scissors

plain paper

masking tape

rubber (latex) gloves

silkscreen cleaner

soft cloths

protective face mask

clear car spray lacquer

1 Choose a moulding with a wide, flat face. Cut the printed text into strips and place it face down on plain paper, securing it with masking tape. Wearing rubber (latex) gloves, pour a small amount of silkscreen cleaner on to a piece of cloth. Gently wipe the cloth over the back of the paper bearing the text. Then, using a dry cloth, wipe over the photocopy again to transfer a reverse image of the text on to the plain paper.

2 Secure the reversed text to the frame text side down, using masking tape. Gently apply silkscreen cleaner to the paper. Using a dry cloth, wipe over the paper. Remove the applied text and leave to dry for 10 minutes.

3 Transfer the text all around the frame. Wearing a protective face mask, apply a coat of car spray lacquer over the frame to seal the lettering.

This attractive decoupage frame makes use of black and white photocopies of images, which are then coloured with paint. The shellac lends an antique colour to the frame.

Decoupage Frame

you will need
2.5cm/1in flat sable paintbrush
acrylic gesso
wooden frame, prepared and sanded
fine-grade sandpaper
(glasspaper)
yellow ochre pigment
photocopied designs
craft knife
cutting mat
round sable paintbrush
watercolour paints
PVA (white) glue
spray lacquer
2.5cm/1in lacquer paintbrush
shellac
white spirit (paint thinner)
fine and extra-fine wet-and-dry
paper
cork sanding block, optional
soft cloths
metal polish

1 Using a flat sable paintbrush, apply acrylic gesso over the frame. Allow to dry, then apply another four coats of gesso, allowing each coat to dry before applying the next. Allow to dry. Gently sand the surface with fine-grade sandpaper (glasspaper).

2 Combine 1.5ml/¼ tsp yellow ochre pigment with 30ml/2 tbsp water and blend thoroughly until no flecks of pigment are visible in the mixture. Using the flat sable paintbrush, apply two coats of the mixture over the frame. Allow to dry.

3 Photocopy the designs you wish to use from a book or magazine. Accurately cut out each shape with a craft knife, working on a cutting mat.

4 Using a round sable paintbrush, paint the photocopies with watercolour paints.

5 Glue the photocopied cut-outs to the frame using PVA (white) glue. Press them down carefully to remove air bubbles. Leave to dry.

6 Apply a coat of spray lacquer over the cut-outs. This will stop the paint on the photocopies bleeding into the coloured frame. Leave to dry.

7 Use a lacquer brush to apply ten coats of shellac to the frame, allowing each to dry before applying the next. Once the shellac is completely dry, rub the frame down with white spirit (paint thinner). Use wet-and-dry paper and a cork sanding block if the frame is flat, and finish with a finer wet-and-dry paper. Wipe off excess white spirit with a dry cloth. Apply a pea-sized amount of metal polish to a cloth and polish all around the frame. Buff up with a clean dry cloth.

In this striking design, a feather is sandwiched between two sheets of glass which are edged in lead. You may also wish to gild the outer area of glass using the verre eglomisé technique, (see page 111).

Lead Frame

you will need

2 pieces of glass

cloth

methylated spirits (denatured alcohol)

4 wood fillets, 5mm/¼in thick

pencil

craft knife or hacksaw

cutting mat

thick black marker pen

epoxy resin glue

bradawl (awl)

nylon thread

feather or other lightweight object

weight

protective gloves

scissors, optional

self-adhesive lead

plastic smoothing tool

self-adhesive hangers

1 Clean the glass thoroughly with a cloth dipped in methylated spirits (denatured alcohol). Measure the wood fillets against the sides of one piece of glass and mark with a pencil where they are to be cut.

2 Once the fillets have been measured and marked, cut along the pencil line with a craft knife on a cutting mat. Alternatively, use a hacksaw with a thin blade.

3 Colour the fillets all over with a thick black marker pen. Using epoxy resin glue, stick the blackened fillets around three sides of one piece of glass, leaving the top section open.

4 Using a bradawl (awl), make a small hole in the remaining fillet and pass a length of nylon thread through it. Secure this. On the other end of the nylon thread, stick the feather with epoxy resin glue.

 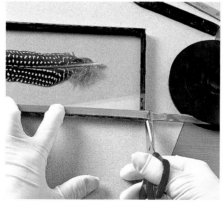 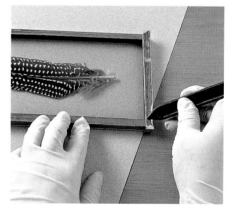

5 Centre the feather in the frame and stick the remaining top fillet to the glass. Place small drops of epoxy resin glue on all four fillets then place the second piece of glass on top. Leave to set for approximately 10–15 minutes, preferably with a weight on top.

6 Wearing protective gloves and using scissors or a craft knife, cut self-adhesive lead strips to the size of the glass edges, just overlapping each edge.

7 Warm the lead strip in the palm of your hand for a few seconds. Remove the backing strip, place the lead strip on the glass edge and apply pressure with a plastic smoothing tool. Trim off the excess. Continue all around the frame. Attach self-adhesive hangers to the back of the frame.

Glass is required on any artwork needing protection from atmospheric pollution and ultraviolet rays, which in time will cause a picture to fade. Different types of glass suit different framing purposes.

Choosing Glass

The type of glass used in picture framing is known as float glass, which is of a higher quality and clarity than sheet glass which is normally used for glazing windows and doors. The most commonly used is 2mm/1⁄16in thick. For more precious artwork, museum glass is used; although extremely expensive, it is the best protection for artwork and it is almost invisible.

Clear glass

The staple glass for picture framing, clear glass is generally 2mm/1⁄16in thick, which is the optimum thickness for strength and ease of cutting. This glass has a shiny surface that reflects light and causes a mirror-effect in some situations. For reasons of safety, 2mm/1⁄16 in glass is used only up to a certain size, approximately 1m/1⁄8yd across. For areas larger than this, heavy-duty glass 4–6mm/1⁄8–1⁄4in thick should be used.

Non-reflective glass

This has a slightly frosted or cloudy appearance because one side of the glass is etched with hydrochloric acid to create a surface that breaks up the reflected light. As only 87 per cent of transmitted light passes through the glass, the image becomes increasingly diffused if it is mounted in a double or triple mount (mat).

Anti-reflective glass

This glass allows 98 per cent of transmitted light to pass through. It is almost invisible over artwork and as a result is sometimes known as "magic" glass. Its anti-reflective properties are effective from all angles.

Perspex (plexiglass)

Clear acrylic sheet is a lightweight, non-breakable alternative to clear glass. It is ideal for protecting pictures that are to hang in busy public areas, on business premises or in children's rooms where safety is a priority.

Glass suppliers will cut glass to size for you at the time of purchase, but you may also need to cut pieces yourself if you are doing a lot of framing. The skill needs a confident but careful approach.

Cutting Glass

you will need

frame

tape measure

protective cotton gloves

fine black marker pen

picture glass

T-square

glass cutter

piece of board

pencil

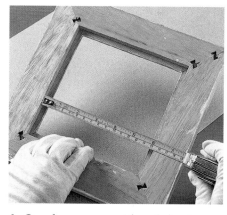

1 On the reverse side of the frame, measure the horizontal from rebate to rebate. Wear protective cotton gloves when you are handling glass.

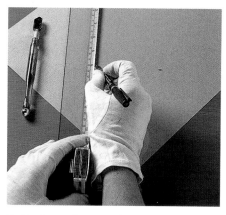

2 Reduce the window measurement by 2mm/¹⁄₁₆in, then mark the measurement on the glass using a fine black marker pen.

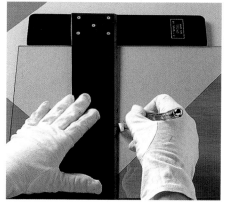

3 Place a T-square on the glass and line up the glass cutter so that it is on top of the marks. Holding both the glass cutter and T-square, firmly score the glass with the glass cutter in one long smooth stroke. Do not cut again over the same line, as this will make the glass shatter and splinter.

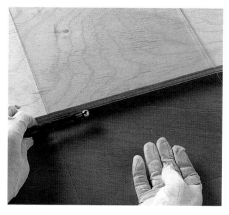

4 Hold the glass over a board so that the score line is on the edge. Gently tap the glass below the score mark, using the round end of the cutter.

5 Place a pencil directly beneath the cut. Using both hands placed on each side of the pencil and score mark, gently but firmly press the glass down. The glass will break cleanly along the score line. Repeat for the vertical measurement. When the glass is cut, clean it, then gently insert it in the rebate at the back of the frame.

"Fitting up" is the process of fixing the artwork into the frame itself. It is advisable to follow the simple steps below and assemble the sections in the correct order.

Fitting up a Frame

you will need
tape measure
frame
pencil
picture glass
glass cutter
protective cotton gloves
fine black marker pen
T-square
piece of board
white sheet
methylated spirits (denatured alcohol)
soft cloth
mounted artwork
backing board
framer's points or panel pins (brads)
point gun or hammer
self-adhesive sealing tape
craft knife
bradawl (awl) or drill and bit
2 D-rings
screwdriver
picture hanging wire
wire cutters

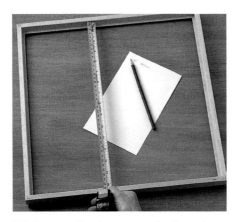

1 Measure the frame inside the rebate horizontally and vertically. Take 2mm/1⁄16 in from each measurement to find the finished glass size. Cut the glass to size.

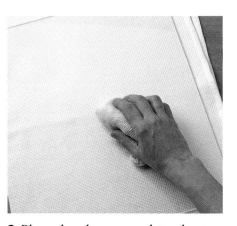

2 Place the glass on a white sheet so that you can see any blemishes more easily. Clean both sides of the glass with methylated spirits (denatured alcohol) and buff with a soft cloth.

3 Place the mounted artwork on top of the backing board and place the glass on top. Lower the frame on to the glass. Pick up the assembled frame and check that there are no flecks of dust under the glass.

4 Turn the entire frame over and place face down on a folded sheet. Insert framer's points or panel pins (brads) on each side of the frame using a point gun or a hammer. Insert pins near each corner and then one or two in between, approximately 8–10cm/3–4in apart.

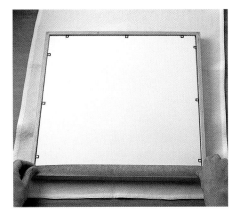

5 Cut the end of the self-adhesive sealing tape straight. Stick the first length down along the first side so that it is approximately 3mm/⅛in away from the edge. Using a craft knife, cut the tape at the other end parallel to the edge of the frame.

6 Turn the frame around. Lay the next length of tape exactly overlapping the end of the first strip and stick along the next edge. Cut the tape off at the end 3mm/⅛in away from the outside edge of the frame. Repeat on the remaining two sides.

7 From the top edge of the picture, measure one-third of the way down each side and mark with a pencil. Use a bradawl (awl) to make a hole or drill a small guide hole at each mark.

8 Choose the size of D-ring fastening to fit within the width of the moulding. Screw a D-ring into the frame at each guide hole.

9 Wrap picture hanging wire twice around the first D-ring and then twist the end around the hanging wire six or seven times so that the coils are tightly packed. The hanging wire should be long enough to go round two widely spaced hooks positioned just below the top of the picture.

10 Tie off the wire around the second D-ring in the same way and cut off the excess wire. Hang the picture from two widely spaced hooks. The wire should rise almost vertically from the D-rings to put the least amount of strain on the frame.

Fillets can be used in picture framing to create a space between the glass and a three-dimensional artwork. Plain wood strips can be used, but the fillets will be visible and should match the frame or the artwork.

Adding Fillets

you will need
tape measure
frame
narrow batten
pencil
cutting mat
craft knife
picture glass
PVA (white) glue and brush

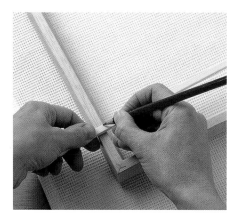

1 Measure across the top of the reverse side of the frame from one side of the rebate to the other. Mark this measurement on the length of batten you are using for the fillets.

2 Lay the batten on a cutting mat and cut to size with a sturdy craft knife. Cut a second piece for the bottom of the frame. Fit these two fillets in the frame then mark and cut two side pieces to fit between them.

3 Place the glass in the frame. Spread glue along the top and bottom pieces of fillet and fit into the frame. Spread glue on the side pieces and stick in position. The side pieces should fit snugly with a neat join at each corner. Leave to dry before inserting the artwork and fitting up the frame.

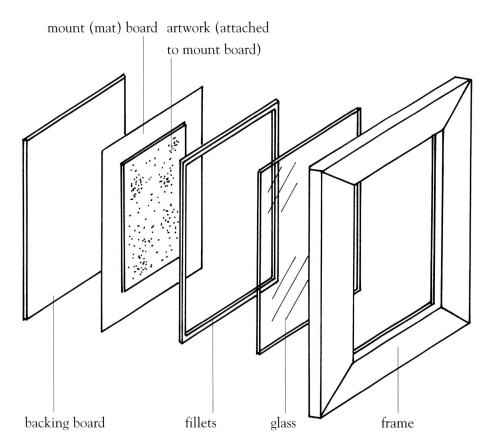

mount (mat) board   artwork (attached to mount board)

backing board   fillets   glass   frame

Picture placement is an art in itself. To conserve your artworks, avoid hanging them near heat sources or in direct sunlight, and never under-estimate the weight of a framed picture.

Hanging Pictures

▲ A muted interior is enhanced by this casually placed picture.

▼ Small pictures make a stronger statement if hung as a group.

▲ Hang pictures at a lower level if you usually view them sitting down.

▼ Framed pictures can be heavy. Invest in proper picture wire cord and fixtures of adequate strength.

Paint Effects

You can use a wide range of paint effects to brighten and transform existing picture frames. A simple coat of colourwash or woodstain will add instant colour while still allowing the grain of the wood to show through, or you could go for a more dramatic look, such as gilding or a tortoiseshell effect, to create sumptuous style. Add extra decoration with stencils or stamps, and finish with wax or varnish to protect your work.

Playing with Colour

Paint is the most basic material to choose when decorating frames. It comes in any colour you want, it is easy to use, and it creates an immediate impression. However, you don't need to use just paint. You could also try woodstain as an instant dilute covering for wood; ink for penwork decoration; wax, tinted or plain, for a soft sheen; varnish, tinted for an aged look; and glaze to create some of the more complicated effects.

This chapter features a selection of ideas for decorating your frames with paint, glazes and varnish, ranging from the quick and easy to the more

sophisticated and time-consuming. So take a look through and have a go at some of the projects. Paint is versatile, and if your first attempt goes wrong, you can simply paint over the top and start again.

Colourwashing and woodstaining are two easy paint effects, both of which use dilute mixes of paint and stain to cover a wooden frame; as the wash and stain are so dilute, the grain of the wood still shows through. You could add further to this

effect, perhaps by gluing extra decoration over the top, or adding penwork or painted motifs. Alternatively you could stencil repeat motifs around the frame, using the colourwash as a background. Other paint techniques include marbling and tor-

toiseshell effects, both of which can be achieved using paint glazes and a little patience. Remember that you are not aiming at an absolute reproduction of marble or tortoiseshell, merely a decorative effect, so don't be nervous about these techniques.

Gilding is another very effective method of transforming a frame. You can cover the frame completely with gold or Dutch metal leaf, or simply apply

squares or cut-out shapes of leaf to the corners or sides of the frame. Then you can distress the gilding for an antiqued effect, or simply seal it to prevent it tarnishing. Paint effects should always be sealed with wax or varnish to protect the surface and make the decoration more durable. Wax provides less protection but gives a softer sheen, whereas varnish is more hardwearing, though not as subtle.

The list below includes the paint and other materials required for the projects in this chapter. Specialist equipment, such as gilder's brushes and metal foils, is available from art and framing suppliers.

Materials and Equipment

Epoxy putty
This strong, two-part putty adheres well and can be used to fill small cracks when restoring old frames.

Gelatine capsules
When melted in hot water, these capsules produce an adhering solution for use in the glass-gilding technique known as verre eglomisé.

Gilder's cushion
Used for preparing and cutting loose gold leaf.

Gilder's knife
The knife has a long straight blade for cutting loose gold leaf on a cushion.

Gilder's tip
This wide brush is used for lifting loose leaf on to a sized surface. Wipe it across your face or a smear of petroleum jelly to pick up a little grease before touching it to the leaf.

Gold leaf
Real gold leaf is expensive but produces unrivalled gilding and can be burnished to a bright gleam. It is supplied loose in "books" of 25 sheets.

Acrylic gesso
Use gesso to provide a smooth base on the surface of the frame before applying painted or gilded decoration. It should be built up in a series of thin coats, and when hard can be sanded to porcelain smoothness or carved and incised in very fine detail.

Agate burnisher
This traditional gilder's tool is used to polish gilding over a gesso surface to a brilliant shine.

Dutch metal leaf
Imitation gold or silver leaf is available either loose or on transfer sheets. It needs to be protected with varnish to prevent tarnishing.

Epoxy glue
This resin glue is a very strong two-part adhesive used to join materials such as metal, stone and glass. Once mixed, it sets in 20 minutes. Mix as much as you need on a piece of scrap card which you can then dispose of.

Liming wax
This consists of clear wax mixed with whiting that collects in wood grain to give a pale limed effect.

Metal polish

This is a fine abrasive cream. It may be used on any surface coated with shellac to give a glossy appearance.

Methylated spirits (denatured alcohol)

This solvent is used as a thinner for woodstain and to clean paintbrushes and glass.

Paint

Gouache is a very opaque, water-based paint that gives a professional finish. **Acrylic** paints are also water-based and are more translucent than gouache. **Oil** paints can be used as a finish, or rubbed into wood grain or a craquelure varnish. **Emulsion (latex)** paint is quick-drying and a good base coat for large projects. **Black patina** is used to give an aged look. **Chalkboard** paint gives a matt black finish.

Paintbrushes

Use sable and flat oil paintbrushes for decoration, household brushes for applying primer and varnishing brushes for protective finishes.

Pigments

These are the purest form of paint and are extremely strong. Use them to tint other media.

Pumice powder

A fine powder abrasive that can be used for distressing gilded surfaces. Different grades are available.

Sandpaper (glasspaper)

Available in different grades, from fine to coarse. Wet-and-dry sandpaper can be rinsed free of dust, making it reusable and longer-lasting. Wrap sandpaper around a cork sanding block when smoothing flat surfaces.

Self-adhesive lead strip

Available in different widths and sold in most hardware stores. It is designed to imitate the lead dividers in stained glass windows.

Shellac

Also known as special pale polish or button polish and used on wood. It is quick-drying and can be tinted to give an antique effect.

Silicone rubber

Cold-curing silicone can be used to make flexible moulds for restoring damaged frame mouldings.

Size

Used in gilding as a mordant. **Oil** size is available with different drying times: the longer the drying time, the shinier the gilding. **Acrylic** size can be used with Dutch metal leaf.

Spray lacquer

Car spray lacquer is available clear or coloured from car maintenance retailers. Work in a well-ventilated area and wear a safety mask.

Stamps

Decorative rubber stamps are available in many designs, or you can make your own from medium density foam.

Stencil card (card stock)

Thin cardboard treated to make it strong and reusable.

Tape

Use masking tape to define areas when painting designs, and to protect mirrors when decorating their frames.

Varnishes

Acrylic varnishes are available in different sheens from high gloss to matt, and have a much faster drying time than spirit (alcohol)-based varnishes. **Craquelure** is a two-part varnish which produces a crackled effect. **Sanding sealer** is quick-drying.

Wax

Clear wax is used to coat and enrich wood. Picture framer's gilt wax is used to disguise repairs to old gilt frames.

White spirit (paint thinner)

This solvent is used for oil size, and for cleaning brushes when using any oil-based products.

Wire (steel) wool

Used for rubbing down and distressing painted or gilded surfaces, and for applying liming wax.

Wood glue

PVA (white) wood glue is used for securing joints in wood.

Woodfiller

Used to fill in gaps on mitred corners and after punching nails into wood. Various types of filler are available.

Woodstain

Available in an abundance of colours and types, from crystals to solutions. Woodstain can be bought from art shops and hardware stores.

Wooden frames are easy to decorate and restore, and can be transformed with many different types of paint finish and decorative paint effects. Gilding is a traditional and beautiful method of decoration.

Paint Techniques

Restoration

Damaged frames need not always be consigned to the rubbish heap. Missing parts of the moulding can be replaced by making plaster casts.

1 Mix some cold-curing silicone, adding curing agent at the ratio of 1 part curing agent to 20 parts silicone base. Mix a small amount of thixotropic additive into the mixture. Once it is the consistency of whipped cream, spread it on to a clean, undamaged section of frame identical to the missing part. Leave to dry for 24 hours, then remove the mould.

2 When the mould is dry, fill it two-thirds full with water then empty the water into a jug. Sprinkle casting plaster into the water until the plaster sits on top and the water no longer absorbs it. Stir thoroughly. Pour the plaster mixture into the mould, and allow to dry for 1 hour. Peel the mould away from the plaster. Trim the cast and fit it in the damaged area of the frame.

Gilding

Traditional gilding techniques using loose gold leaf demand a high degree of skill. Transfer imitation leaf is cheaper and easier to manage.

1 Build up a smooth surface for gilding with several coats of gesso or, if using Dutch metal leaf, prepare with red oxide primer. Apply a thin even coat of oil or water-based size to the primed surface, avoiding air bubbles, and leave to become tacky.

2 If you are using loose metal leaf, open the book over a gilder's pad and blow the leaf on to the pad. Ensure the leaf is flat but do not touch it. Brush a gilder's tip over your face or over a smear of petroleum jelly. Touch the tip on the leaf to lift it from the cushion.

3 Use the gilder's tip to touch the leaf to the sized surface, keeping the tip almost parallel with the surface. The leaf will be pulled down by capillary action. Tamp it down gently with cotton wool (cotton balls) to eliminate any air bubbles.

4 If you are using transfer leaf, position the leaf on the sized surface, slightly overlapping the previous one, and rub over the backing paper until the leaf adheres. Lift the paper.

5 Repeat until the whole area is covered. Brush away any loose pieces of leaf with a soft brush: you can save these to be reused later to fill any gaps in the gilding.

6 Seal the surface with wax or polish. Add a few drops of polish to a cloth and apply to the frame. Buff the surface when dry.

Finishing a gilded frame

If you feel that a gilded frame is too bright, you can distress or antique the finish, and seal it to prevent it tarnishing. The following techniques are easy ways to achieve a distressed or antiqued look.

Distressing

Antiquing

Sealing

Using fine-grade wire (steel) wool, gently drag it along the leaf in one direction, concentrating on areas that would naturally suffer wear and tear. Moisten a piece of paper towel with white spirit (paint thinner) and gently wipe it over the areas you have distressed, removing the grey particles of wire wool to reveal the undercoat. This can be done as lightly or heavily as you wish. Leave to dry before sealing the surface.

Mix raw umber acrylic paint with a tiny amount of water. Brush it on in one direction, wait a few minutes, then wipe off the surplus with paper towels, wiping in one direction. This leaves a slightly streaky appearance. For a more obviously dragged look, use a slightly dampened flat brush to remove the surplus paint. Allow to dry and then seal.

Use sanding sealer or shellac to seal the leaf and prevent tarnishing. Sanding sealer is virtually colourless, whereas shellac enhances the colour. Brush on an even coat, but try to avoid going over an area twice, or the first layer may start to lift off. Watch for runs and remove them as soon as possible, as both lacquers dry very quickly. Clean the brush immediately in methylated spirits (denatured alcohol). Allow to dry for about an hour.

Paint effects Many decorative paint effects can be used to rejuvenate old frames. Some, such as tortoiseshell, can look very striking and dramatic, while others, such as colourwashing, have a more subtle effect.

Preparation

Frames should always be prepared before a new paint effect is applied. First, remove the old paint and varnish using a proprietary paint stripper and scraper. It is best to work outdoors or in a well-ventilated room as the fumes can be very strong. Then wash the frame with warm soapy water and a sponge and allow to dry. Finally, rub the frame down with sandpaper (glasspaper) to remove the last traces of old paint and to smooth the surface ready for the new treatment.

Colourwash

Dilute water-based paint and mix thoroughly to make a thin wash. Apply the wash over the frame with a paintbrush, using a single, long, even stroke on each section of the frame. Allow to dry. The wood grain should remain visible beneath the colour.

Liming wax

Liming wax is a mixture of wax and white pigment and can be applied over either a painted or unpainted frame to provide a subtle whitening effect, especially if the wood of the frame is open-grained. Rub the wax into the frame using wire (steel) wool.

Picture framer's gilt wax

This instant finish is useful for covering repairs. Various different shades are available to match existing gilding. You can also use it to add a hint of gold to painted decoration. Apply gilt wax over either a painted or unpainted frame with your finger, then buff with a soft cloth to increase the shine.

Woodstain

Woodstain will colour a wooden frame without concealing the grain of the wood, unlike paint. It is a dilute wash that dries quickly. Apply woodstain with a paintbrush, in even strokes.

Tortoiseshell

This sumptuous paint effect aims to imitate the translucent look of real tortoiseshell. It is achieved by applying diagonal strokes of thin oil glazes in raw umber, burnt sienna and black between many layers of clear shellac varnish. The frame is first gilded to reflect light through the varnish.

Ageing techniques

These techniques create an old, faded look, imitating the effects of time and age on the surface. To look authentic, distressing should concentrate on areas where wear and tear would normally occur.

Distressing

Using fine-grade sandpaper (glasspaper), gently rub down a painted frame to remove some of the paint and reveal the wood beneath. Work carefully, so the distressing is even and not too patchy. Pay particular attention to the corners of the frame.

Using crackle varnish

1 Brush a generous, even coat of the first stage of the crackle varnish over the surface. Check that the surface is completely covered, then leave to dry for 1–3 hours. Test it by lightly touching the varnish with your fingers; it should feel dry but slightly tacky.

3 If no cracks have appeared, speed up the drying process by moving a hairdryer on its coolest setting over the surface, but not too close to the varnish. Stop as soon as cracks appear. If you are unhappy with the finished effect, remove the varnish with a cloth soaked in water and start again.

2 Brush on a layer of the second stage of the varnish, working evenly and in one direction. Leave to dry for 1–2 hours. Hold the frame up to the light to see if any cracks have appeared: the reaction time will depend on the temperature and humidity of the room in which you are working.

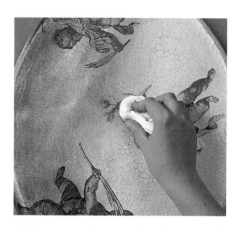

4 Mix raw umber artist's oil paint with a little white spirit (paint thinner). Wipe this mixture in a circular motion all over the surface using paper towels or a soft cloth. Wipe off surplus paint with a clean piece of paper towel, so that the colour is just left in the cracks. Leave to dry thoroughly. Finish with 1–2 layers of oil-based varnish.

Stencils and stamps Making your own stencils is not difficult, and a lot cheaper than buying ready-cut designs. It is also easy to make your own stamps using high or medium density foam, or even a household sponge.

Transferring a design

1 To transfer a template on to a piece of stencil card (card stock), place a piece of tracing paper over the design, and draw over it with a hard pencil.

2 On the back of the design rub over the lines with a soft pencil. Turn the tracing to the right side and place on top of a sheet of stencil card. Draw over the lines with a hard pencil.

Making a stencil

1 Place the stencil card (card stock) on a cutting mat or piece of thick cardboard and tape in place. Use a craft knife for cutting.

2 It is safer to turn the cutting board as you work so that you are always drawing the knife towards you when cutting around awkward shapes.

Making a stamp

1 Draw a simple design on to a household sponge using a marker pen.

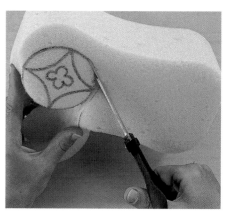

2 Cut around the outline of the design with a pair of sharp scissors. Cut away the unwanted background areas with a craft knife when the outline has been cut. Rinse the completed stamp to remove the remains of the marker ink.

Finishing techniques

Varnish is more hardwearing than wax and gives a matt or glossy finish. Wax offers less protection but it can be replenished from time to time and gives the surface a soft sheen.

Waxing

In addition to providing a protective coating, wax adds a decorative finish. You can use antiquing wax to darken the surface and achieve the look of mahogany or other wood. Apply the wax with a soft cloth and rub it into the wood of the frame, then buff up with a cloth for a soft sheen.

Varnish

Stir the varnish well before using. Coat the brush about halfway up the bristles and lay the varnish on in light strokes, working in one direction. Do not apply too much varnish at a time as this can cause runs. Apply several coats for a protective finish.

Shellac

Shellac can be used to seal bare wood prior to varnishing or painting to prevent the wood from discolouring. It can also be used to seal metal leaf to prevent it tarnishing. Apply shellac with a soft brush or cloth. It will dry very quickly.

Washing brushes

After using paintbrushes, they should always be cleaned straight away. Wash brushes in soapy water if you have been using water-based paint, then rinse in running water, always holding the bristles downwards so they are not damaged by the stream of water. If you have been using oil-based paint or varnish, clean brushes with methylated spirits (denatured alcohol) to remove the paint or varnish.

If your wooden frame has an attractive grain, this simple technique allows you to introduce colour without obscuring the wood's natural qualities. Gouache, acrylic or emulsion (latex) paints are suitable.

Colourwashed Frame

you will need

gouache paint: spectrum violet

bowl

2.5cm/1in flat sable paintbrush

ash or oak frame, prepared and sanded

fine-grade sandpaper (glasspaper)

cloth

clear wax

hardboard offcut (scrap)

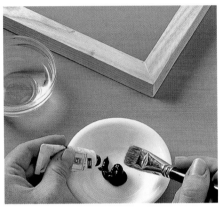

1 Place a walnut-sized amount of violet gouache in a bowl, add a little water and blend in thoroughly. The more water you add, the more translucent the wash will be; if you want a strong colour, add less water. Test the strength of the wash on the back of the frame. When you have the correct dilution, dip a paintbrush into the paint then wipe it against the side of the bowl, removing excess paint.

2 Apply the wash to one section of the face of the frame in one smooth, even stroke, from mitre to mitre. Then paint the side section of the frame. Continue all around the frame. Leave to dry for at least 15 minutes. The more coats of wash applied, the more opaque the colour will appear. Two coats are recommended. Allow to dry.

◄ **3** Lightly sand the frame with fine-grade sandpaper (glasspaper) to distress the wash and give a smooth finish. For a wax finish, cover your finger with a cloth, dip it in wax and work it in on a small piece of hardboard to soften the wax. With one long, smooth stroke lightly apply the wax to the frame; do not rub it in as it may remove the wash. Continue all around the frame. Once finished, lightly rub in the wax from where you began. Two or three coats of wax may be necessary.

This project combines all the creative possibilities of stamping. It involves four processes: painting the background, stamping in one colour, over-printing in a second colour and rubbing back.

Stamped Star Frame

you will need

wooden frame, prepared and sanded

emulsion (latex) paint: sky blue, red-brown and gold

paintbrush

palette or plate

foam roller

small and large star stamps

fine wire (steel) wool

1 Paint the frame blue and leave to dry. Put some red-brown paint on a palette and run a foam roller through it until evenly coated. Use the roller to ink a small star stamp and print it in the middle of each side of the frame.

2 Using the red-brown paint, stamp a large star over each corner of the frame. Leave to dry.

3 Ink the large stamp with gold and over-print the corner stars. Allow to dry before rubbing the frame gently with wire (steel) wool.

The stylish raised leaf patterns around this pair of frames are simple to create using white interior filler to fill in stencilled shapes. Why not make several matching frames using different combinations of motifs?

Leaf-stippled Frames

you will need

2 wooden frames, prepared and sanded

acrylic paint: dark green

paintbrush

fine-grade sandpaper (glasspaper)

paper

pencil

stencil card (card stock)

scissors

ready-mixed interior filler

stencil brush

1 Paint the frames dark green. When dry, gently rub them down to create a distressed effect. Enlarge the templates at the back of the book to fit the frames, transfer them to stencil card (card stock) and cut them out.

2 Position a stencil on one of the frames and stipple ready-mixed filler through it using a stencil brush. Reposition the stencil and repeat. Continue all round the frame, spacing the leaves evenly. Leave to dry.

3 Repeat with a different combination of motifs on the second frame. When the filler is completely hard, gently smooth the leaves with fine-grade sandpaper (glasspaper).

Three-dimensional motifs applied on the face of a picture frame are simple to create using interior filler. Tint the filler any colour you choose by adding pigment, gouache or watercolour paint.

Raised Motif Frame

you will need
bowls
gouache paint: cobalt blue
2.5cm/1in flat sable paintbrush
wooden frame, prepared and sanded
fine-grade sandpaper (glasspaper)
tracing paper
pencil
stencil card (card stock)
cutting mat
craft knife
interior filler
pigment
stencil brush

1 In a bowl, blend one part cobalt blue gouache paint with three parts water. Paint this wash on to the frame in long, even strokes, working from mitre to mitre. Leave to dry for approximately 15 minutes.

2 Lightly distress the face and edges of the frame by rubbing them with fine-grade sandpaper (glasspaper).

3 Trace the design for the frame using the template at the back of the book, then transfer on to stencil card (card stock). Place this on a cutting mat and cut out the design with a craft knife.

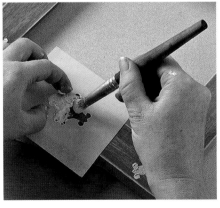

4 Mix two parts interior filler with one part water and mix to an ice cream consistency. Add pigment to tint the filler. Place the stencil on the frame and hold securely. Apply the filler by stippling with a stencil brush.

5 Lift off the stencil and repeat all round the frame. Leave the filler to dry for approximately 30 minutes, then lightly smooth the surface using fine-grade sandpaper.

This frame is made from an old plank sawn into pieces and simply glued together. The paint and stencil are applied and then rubbed back to produce an antique effect.

Framed Chalkboard

you will need

spray adhesive

stencil card (card stock)

craft knife and cutting mat

wooden frame, prepared and sanded

emulsion (latex) paint: blue and red

small paintbrush

medium-grade sandpaper (glasspaper)

artist's acrylic paint: black

stencil brush

antiquing varnish

varnish brush

hardboard, cut 2.5cm/1in larger all around than the inner frame measurement

chalkboard paint

hammer

panel pins (brads)

1 Photocopy the templates provided at the back of the book. Spray the back of each with adhesive and stick on to stencil card (card stock). Cut out the shapes.

2 Paint the frame with an even coat of blue emulsion (latex) paint. Leave the frame to dry.

3 Paint the inner and outer edges of the frame red. Leave to dry.

4 Rub the paint with sandpaper (glasspaper) to reveal the grain of the wood.

5 Spray the back of each stencil lightly with spray adhesive and place on the frame.

6 Darken the red paint by mixing in a little black acrylic paint. Using a stencil brush, stipple red paint through the stencils to produce an even covering of paint. Practise first on the wrong side of the frame if you are unfamiliar with the technique.

7 Using the stencil brush, rub the dark red paint deep into the grain in just a few places.

8 When dry, rub over with sandpaper (glasspaper) to remove any dark red paint from the surface.

9 Apply a coat of antiquing varnish. Leave to dry.

10 Paint the hardboard with two coats of chalkboard paint. Leave to dry. Fix the chalkboard to the back of the frame, using panel pins (brads).

Adorn an old gilded frame with gilded and coloured seashells to give it a baroque look. Shells are ideal objects for gilding, as the added lustre brings out their beautiful natural detail.

Gilded Shell Frame

you will need
assorted seashells
red oxide spray primer
1cm/½in paintbrushes
water-based size
Dutch metal leaf: gold and aluminium
soft brush
amber shellac
acrylic varnish
acrylic paints: pale blue, pink and orange
soft cloths
gilded frame
strong clear glue

1 Spray the shells with an even coat of red oxide spray primer and leave to dry for 30–60 minutes. Paint on a thin, even coat of water-based size and leave for 20–30 minutes, until it becomes clear and tacky.

2 Gild the shells with gold or aluminium Dutch metal leaf, dabbing the leaf into place with a soft brush. Use the brush to remove any excess leaf.

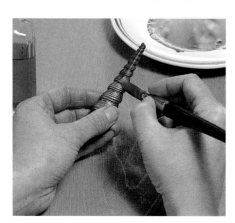

3 Seal the gold shells with a thin, even coat of amber shellac and leave to dry for 45–60 minutes. Seal the aluminium-leaf covered shells with acrylic varnish and leave to dry for at least an hour.

4 Mix some pale blue acrylic paint with a little water. Paint on to the shells, then rub off most of the paint with a cloth, allowing only a little paint to remain in the recessed areas. Colour some of the shells in pink and orange. Leave to dry for 30 minutes.

5 Arrange the shells on the gilded frame and attach in place with strong clear glue. Leave to dry thoroughly before hanging the frame.

This distressed effect is achieved using a wax resist technique. The wax prevents the top coat of paint adhering in places, so that it can be rubbed away to reveal the second colour beneath.

Distressed Mirror Frame

you will need

mirror with wooden frame, prepared and sanded

masking tape

emulsion (latex) paint: white, light green and blue

paintbrush

soft cloth

wax polish

sandpaper (glasspaper)

1 Protect the mirror with masking tape. Paint the frame with white emulsion (latex) paint, then apply a coat of light green emulsion. Leave to dry.

2 Using a cloth, rub wax polish over the surface of the frame. Leave to dry. Paint a coat of blue emulsion paint over the frame and leave to dry.

3 When the paint is dry, rub sandpaper (glasspaper) over the whole surface to reveal some of the colour beneath. Remove the masking tape.

Faux verdigris is achieved by using green and metallic acrylic paints to simulate the green deposit that forms on copper or brass which has become oxidized after exposure to the elements.

Verdigris Frame

you will need
wooden frame, prepared and sanded
acrylic paint: iridescent copper, emerald green, white and black
paintbrush
soft cloth

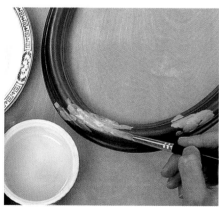

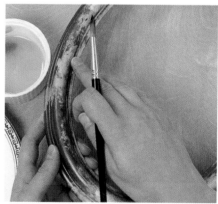

1 Paint the frame with iridescent copper acrylic paint. When dry, mix emerald green with white and paint in random patches on to the copper.

2 While the paint is wet, remove some of the green colour with a cloth, to create a textured look.

3 Paint on some small areas of black acrylic and rub the paint in with your fingers. Leave to dry.

Liming wax is usually applied to attractively grained wood such as oak or ash. The white pigment in the mixture settles into the grain of the wood, while the wax on the surface remains translucent.

Lime-waxed Frame

you will need

wooden frame, prepared and sanded

coarse- and fine-grade sandpaper (glasspaper)

liming wax

wire (steel) wool

cloth

1 Sand the frame all over, initially with coarse-grade then with fine-grade sandpaper, to give a smooth surface.

2 Pick up some liming wax on a piece of wire (steel) wool and apply it to the frame in long even strokes, continuing all around the frame. Work the wax into the wood grain as you go. Apply a second coat of liming wax to achieve a deeper effect.

3 When you have covered the frame completely, gently polish the liming wax with a cloth. Do not use excessive pressure as this will wipe off too much of the wax.

Woodstain penetrates the wood but allows the grain to show through, giving a translucent finish. Brushes should be cleaned with methylated spirits (denatured alcohol) when using a spirit-based stain.

Woodstained Frame

you will need

wooden frame, prepared and sanded

spirit (alcohol)-based woodstain

methylated spirits (denatured alcohol)

glass bowl

rubber (latex) gloves

2.5cm/1in flat sable paintbrush

acrylic varnish and brush

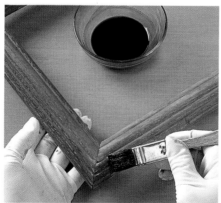

1 For an opaque result, use pure undiluted woodstain. For a translucent finish, dilute the woodstain with methylated spirits (denatured alcohol). Decant the mixture into a glass bowl. Wear rubber (latex) gloves when working with woodstain.

2 Dip the paintbrush into the solution, wiping off the excess. Apply the stain, working from mitre to mitre, in a single long, even stroke. Repeat all around the sides of the frame. Leave to dry for 10–15 minutes. Two or three coats may be required.

3 When the woodstain is dry to the touch, apply a coat of acrylic varnish. Leave to dry before applying one or two more coats as required.

With the help of a template and tracing paper, you can handpaint a frame to look as good as if it was painted by an artist. Luscious grapes and vine leaves decorate this frame.

Painted Vine Mirror Frame

you will need

masking tape

wooden frame, prepared and sanded, with mirror

paintbrush

emulsion (latex) paint: white

pencil

tracing paper

coloured chalk

acrylic paint: purple, sap green, white and raw umber

artist's brushes

oak-coloured antique varnish

cloth

1 Stick masking tape around the edges of the mirror. Paint the frame with three coats of white emulsion (latex) paint. Trace the grape design provided at the back of the book. Rub chalk on to the back of the tracing. Place the design on a corner of the frame and go over the lines with the pencil, to transfer the design on to the frame. Repeat with the other corners.

2 Dilute the purple and green acrylic paints with water. Using a fine artist's brush, paint a wash of purple for the grapes and green for the leaves on the design. Add white highlights on the grapes and leaves.

3 Paint an outline around the fruit and leaves with raw umber paint using a very fine brush. When dry, apply a coat of antique varnish and rub off any excess with a cloth, to create an antiqued effect.

The uneven markings and crazing that occur naturally in marble can be imitated very convincingly by the skilful application of paint, using just a brush and a feather.

Marble-effect Mirror Frame

you will need

wooden frame, prepared and sanded, with mirror

masking tape

white eggshell paint

paintbrush

oil paint: raw umber, sap green and white

turpentine

linseed oil

cloth

goose feather

soft brush

1 Protect the mirror with masking tape and paint the frame with white eggshell. Thin raw umber and green paint with turpentine and linseed oil. Paint on the frame and take off the excess with a cloth for a textured look.

2 Dip the end of the feather into the green paint mixture and the white oil paint. Draw lines on the frame with the feather. Mix some paint in a stronger colour and draw more lines, varying the pressure of the feather.

3 While the paint is still damp, brush over the frame with a soft brush to merge the lines together, producing the marbled effect.

Transform a wooden frame into a gleaming gilded one using Dutch gold leaf, varnish and orange acrylic glaze. Flicking enamel varnish over the frame creates an effective antiqued look.

Good as Gold

you will need

wooden frame, prepared and sanded

red oxide spray primer

paintbrushes

water-based size

Dutch metal leaf: gold

soft brush

wire (steel) wool

methylated spirits (denatured alcohol)

clear shellac

old stiff brush

French enamel varnish

rubber (latex) gloves

acrylic paint: orange

soft cloth

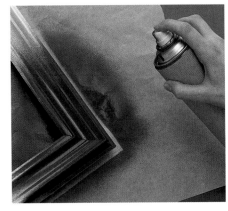

1 Prime the wooden picture frame with the red oxide spray primer. (Use the spray in a well-ventilated room.) Obtain an even coverage and ensure that the wood is completely covered.

2 Apply a thin, but even, coat of water-based size, painting out any bubbles that appear. Leave the size to get tacky, following the manufacturer's instructions on the bottle of size.

3 Place sheets of metal leaf on the size, dabbing them into place with a soft brush. Work around the frame adding leaf, then fill in any tears or gaps.

4 When the surface is completely covered, remove any excess leaf with the soft brush. Using wire (steel) wool and methylated spirits (denatured alcohol), rub over the raised areas to reveal some of the base coat.

5 Apply a coat of shellac to seal the metal leaf and prevent tarnishing.

6 Dip an old, stiff brush into some French enamel varnish and, wearing rubber (latex) gloves, flick the bristles to spray enamel over the frame.

7 When the varnish is dry, dilute some orange acrylic paint with a little water to make a glaze. Paint the glaze all over the frame.

8 While the glaze is still wet, wipe off the excess with a soft cloth so that some paint remains in the detail areas. Allow to dry.

For this striking mirror frame, gold leaf was also used on the frame to create an unusual, unified design. In spite of the delicate appearance of real gold leaf, traditional oil gilding is very hardwearing.

Oil-gilded Frame

you will need
paintbrush
wooden frame, prepared and sanded
gouache paint: ultramarine
white chinagraph pencil
round oil paintbrush
oil size (half-hour drying time)
loose gold leaf
gilder's cushion
gilder's knife
gilder's tip
cotton wool (cotton balls)
soft paintbrush

1 Paint the frame with several coats of ultramarine gouache, allowing each coat to dry completely before applying the next. Draw the design on the frame using a white chinagraph pencil.

2 Using a round oil paintbrush, apply the oil size to the marked shapes. Leave the size to dry for 15–20 minutes, following the manufacturer's instructions, until slightly tacky.

3 Place the gold leaf on a gilder's cushion and cut it into pieces of the appropriate size using a gilder's knife. Brush a gilder's tip over the side of your face to pick up a little grease, then pick up the gold leaf with the tip.

4 Carefully place the gold leaf on the oil-sized design. Leave to dry for another 20 minutes, then gently press the gold leaf down with a pad of cotton wool (cotton ball).

5 After 15–20 minutes, gently wipe off the excess gold leaf with a soft paintbrush or a small pad of cotton wool (cotton ball).

Beautiful old frames can often be found in flea markets, but are usually in need of some restoration. You can restore a frame to its former glory using cold-curing silicone rubber to make a mould for missing details.

Frame Restoration

you will need
damaged gilded frame, cleaned
cold-curing silicone base
curing agent
plastic container
spoon
small spatula
bag of sand
casting plaster
small plastic pot
craft knife
2-part epoxy resin glue
2-part epoxy putty
artist's paintbrush
emulsion (latex) paint: red
picture framer's gilt wax

1 A small area on this frame is missing. Because it is intricately moulded it needs to be copied exactly in order to blend in with the rest of the frame.

2 Mix the cold-curing silicone (see page 76) and spread a thick coat on to an identical area that is clean and not damaged. Remove when dry.

3 Support the rubber mould on a bag loosely filled with sand. Mix a small amount of plaster in a plastic pot (see Techniques) and pour the plaster into the mould. When it is full, shake it slightly to allow any air bubbles to rise. Leave to dry for 2 hours.

4 Remove the cast from the mould and use a craft knife to cut it to the right size to fit the missing area. Stick it to the frame with epoxy resin glue, then leave to dry for 24 hours. Fill any gaps between the cast and the frame with two-part epoxy putty, using a small spatula. Leave to dry for 2 hours.

5 Using an artist's paintbrush, paint the repaired area with red emulsion (latex) paint. Repeat if the plaster is not completely covered by the first coat. Leave to dry for 3 hours. Dip your finger in gilt wax and gently rub it over the red paint. Blend it in carefully at the edges of the repair to match the existing gilding.

This vibrant painted frame, decorated with painted flowers of childlike simplicity, is further enhanced by gilded flourishes sweeping down both sides, which are created using transfer Dutch metal leaf.

Distressed Frame

you will need
acrylic gesso
wooden frame, prepared and sanded
paintbrushes
acrylic paint: ultramarine, cobalt blue, titanium white and cadmium yellow
coarse-grade sandpaper (glasspaper)
cloth
satin acrylic varnish
water-based size
Dutch metal leaf: gold

1 Paint four coats of acrylic gesso on to the frame using a damp paintbrush and allowing the layers to dry between coats. Mix some ultramarine and cobalt blue acrylic paint and paint this over the gesso base coat. Allow to dry.

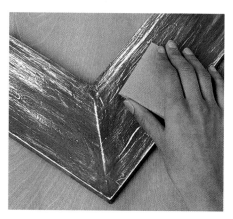

2 Rub back the frame with coarse-grade sandpaper (glasspaper) to create a distressed effect. Buff with a dry cloth. Be careful not to get the gesso wet or it will dissolve. Paint four free-hand daisy flowers in the corners, with white and yellow acrylic paint, using a fine brush. Paint stitches around the edges of the frame in white. When dry, apply a coat of satin varnish to the frame. Allow to dry.

3 To add the gilding, paint two size swirls on to the frame. When the size is tacky, place a piece of Dutch metal leaf on top and rub the backing gently. The leaf will adhere to the size.

This plain wooden frame is simple to make. Choose a wood with an even grain and paint it with a wash of paint. A plain colour will detract less from the item being framed.

Pressed Flowerhead Frame

you will need

pencil
ruler
80cm/32in length of softwood,
7.5cm/3in wide and 2cm/¾in thick
mitre block
saw
wood glue
staple gun
white cardboard
craft knife and cutting mat
wine cork
PVA (white) glue and brush
small paintbrushes
emulsion (latex) paint: white
acrylic paint: pale green and dark blue
artist's paintbrush
pressed scabious flowerhead
double-sided adhesive tape

1 Using a pencil and ruler, mark the softwood into four equal lengths of 20cm/8in, then mark a 45° angle at each end of each length.

2 Place the wood in a mitre block and cut along the marked angles with a saw. These will form the mitres at the corners of the frame.

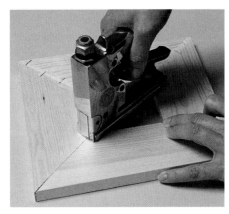

4 Reinforce the glued joins on the reverse side, using a staple gun.

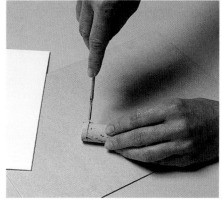

5 Cut a piece of white cardboard the same size as the frame. Using a craft knife, and working on a cutting mat, cut a 1cm/½in slice of cork to support the flowerhead. ▶

3 Glue the four pieces together with wood glue to make a square frame. Leave to dry.

6 Glue the cork support to the centre of the cardboard. This will act as a backing board.

7 Apply two coats of white emulsion (latex) paint to the front of the frame and the backing board, allowing each to dry before applying the next.

8 Take up a little green paint on a dry brush and lightly brush over the frame to leave a trace of paint on the surface.

9 Using an artist's paintbrush, colour the inside and outside edges of the frame with dark blue acrylic paint.

10 Glue the scabious flowerhead to the cork support in the centre of the backing board.

11 Centre the frame over the backing board and hold in place with strips of double-sided adhesive tape.

This modern picture frame is decorated using a simple stencilling technique and treated with a crackle glaze. The brightly coloured paintwork is distressed slightly to give a very attractive finish.

Crackle-glaze Picture Frame

you will need
wooden frame, prepared and sanded
emulsion (latex) paint: yellow ochre,
turquoise, orange, lime green
and bright pink
paintbrushes
acrylic crackle glaze
masking tape
craft knife
flat artist's paintbrush
coarse-grade sandpaper (glasspaper)
acrylic varnish and brush

1 Paint the frame with two coats of yellow ochre emulsion (latex) paint, allowing each to dry. Brush on a coat of crackle glaze. Leave to dry according to the manufacturer's instructions.

2 Place strips of masking tape in a pattern on two opposite sides of the frame, using the finished photograph as your guide.

3 Where the ends of the tape overlap, carefully trim off the excess with a craft knife to leave a straight edge.

4 Brush turquoise paint on some unmasked sections of the frame, working in one direction. The crackle effect will appear almost immediately.

5 Brush orange paint on alternate sections of the pattern in the same way. Paint the remaining sections lime green. Leave the paint to dry, and then carefully peel away the masking tape.

6 Using a flat artist's paintbrush, apply bright pink paint to the areas that were covered by the masking tape. Do this freehand to give the frame a hand-painted look. Leave to dry.

7 Rub coarse-grade sandpaper (glass-paper) over the crackled paint surface to reveal some of the yellow ochre paint beneath.

8 Seal the frame with two coats of acrylic varnish. Apply the first coat quickly, taking care not to overbrush and reactivate the crackle glaze.

A craquelure effect is created using two varnishes. One is slow-drying, while the other is fast-drying. As the slow-drying lower layer contracts it causes cracking in the dry layer of varnish above.

Craquelure Frame

you will need
2.5cm/1in flat sable paintbrush
gouache paint: white
wooden frame, prepared and sanded
fine-grade sandpaper (glasspaper)
clear spray lacquer
2.5cm/1in flat oil paintbrush
two-stage crackle varnish
cloths
palette or plate
oil paint: olive green

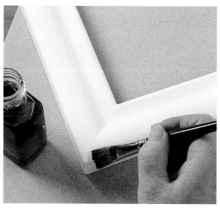

1 With a flat sable paintbrush, apply four coats of white gouache paint to the frame, allowing each to dry before applying the next. Rub over the frame with sandpaper (glasspaper). Spray with clear spray lacquer to make the surface less absorbent.

2 Using a flat oil paintbrush, apply a coat of stage-1 crackle varnish sparingly over the frame. When the varnish has become slightly tacky, apply the stage-2 crackle glaze. Cracks should begin to appear in about an hour. Leave the frame to dry overnight.

3 Wrap your finger in a cloth and dip it into olive green oil paint. Apply the paint all over the frame, working the colour into the cracks. Then wipe the paint off with a cloth; this will remove paint from the surface but leave the colour in the cracks.

Verre eglomisé is glass that has been mirrored using gold or silver leaf, creating a magical, mysterious effect. The technique is named after an eighteenth-century art dealer, Jean-Baptiste Glomy.

Verre Eglomisé Frame

you will need

2.5cm/1in flat oil paintbrush

rubber (latex) gloves

metal polish

wooden frame, prepared and sanded

sponge

black patina

burnishing tool

glass to fit frame

cloths

methylated spirits (denatured alcohol)

gelatine capsules

glass bowl

deep tray

white gold leaf (loose)

gilder's knife

gilder's cushion

2.5cm/1in flat sable paintbrush

gilder's tip

kettle

cotton wool (cotton balls)

pumice powder (0003 grade)

safety mask

black lacquer spray

1 Using a flat oil paintbrush and wearing rubber (latex) gloves, apply metal polish to the frame. Dab the sponge over the polish as you work along the frame for a textured finish. Leave for 30 minutes. Apply a second layer in the same way. Leave overnight to dry.

2 Apply a coat of black patina over the frame, wiping it off as you work. The patina will remain in the recessed areas, giving the impression of age. Leave the frame to dry overnight.

3 Polish the frame with a burnishing tool to give a soft sheen.

4 To create the mirror, clean the glass thoroughly to remove all dirt and grease, using a cloth dipped in methylated spirits (denatured alcohol). ▶

5 Place half a gelatine capsule in a glass bowl and add a little boiling water. When the capsule has completely dissolved, add 300ml/½ pint/ 1¼ cups cold water.

6 Place the glass at an angle of 45° in a deep tray, so that the solution can run down freely. Cut the gold leaf into small squares with a gilder's knife. Using a flat sable paintbrush, apply the solution to the glass and immediately lay a piece of gold leaf on the solution using a gilder's tip.

7 Work from the top to the bottom of the glass. Continue until you have gilded the entire glass, then leave to dry. When the gold leaf looks shiny, it is dry. If it is matt, it is not yet dry.

8 To seal the leaf, hold the gilded glass approximately 20–25cm/8–10in away from the steam of a boiling kettle. Leave to dry. Once dry, gently brush off any excess leaf with cotton wool (cotton balls).

9 A more distressed, antiqued look can be achieved by gently rubbing pumice powder into the gold leaf with your fingertips. When the desired effect has been achieved, brush away the excess powder.

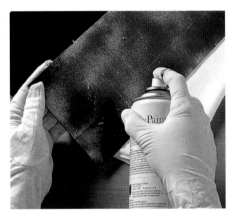

10 Wearing a mask and rubber (latex) gloves, spray black lacquer over the gilded side of the glass. Hold the spray about 20–25cm/8–10in away for an even coat. Leave to dry. Insert the gilded glass in the frame.

This lovely antique-looking mirror, with its intricately moulded frame, has been decorated using the water gilding technique. The delicate finish of this type of gilding is created by building up layers of gesso.

Water-gilded Frame

1 Heat the ready-made white gesso in a bain marie or double boiler for 5 minutes. Paint a coat of gesso on to the picture frame and leave to harden for 1–2 hours.

2 Heat the ready-made red gesso in the same way and paint up to eight thin coats of gesso on to the frame, leaving each coat to dry for 1–2 hours before applying the next one.

3 Paint a thin, even coat of water-based size over the frame and leave for 20–30 minutes until it becomes clear and tacky. Always follow the manufacturer's instructions.

4 Blow a sheet of gold leaf on to a gilder's cushion. Brush a gilder's tip over the side of your face to pick up a little grease, or smear a little petroleum jelly on your arm and brush the tip over it. Touch the tip to the gold leaf to pick up the whole sheet.

5 Lay the leaf on the frame and gently press into place with cotton wool (cotton balls). Repeat until the whole frame is covered.

6 Remove any excess leaf with a soft brush. Leave for 24 hours then burnish the gilding with an agate burnisher. Take care not to rub too hard in case you damage the gesso.

7 To create a distressed effect, gently rub the raised areas with wire (steel) wool to remove a little of the leaf. Take care not to rub too hard.

◄ **8** Make a polishing rubber by wrapping some cotton wool (cotton balls) in a clean rag. Before tying the rag, pour in a little clear shellac to soak the cotton. Tie up the rag with string and, when the shellac soaks through the rag, rub it over the gilding. The surface can be buffed with a soft cloth when dry.

Penwork was one of many artistic amusements popular at the end of the eighteenth century. This elaborately detailed black decoration is traced from a copyright-free book on to a white frame using black ink.

Ink Penwork Frame

you will need

paintbrushes

acrylic gesso

wooden frame, prepared and sanded

medium- and fine-grade sandpaper (glasspaper)

white acrylic paint

tracing paper

design

masking tape

hard and soft pencils

fine black marker pen

emulsion (latex) paint: black

safety mask

clear spray lacquer

2.5cm/1in flat lacquer brush

shellac

1 Apply four coats of acrylic gesso to the frame, allowing it to dry between layers. Sand the gesso with medium-, then fine-grade sandpaper (glasspaper). Apply four layers of white paint to the frame, allowing each coat to dry for 5–10 minutes before applying the next. Place tracing paper over the design. Hold in place with masking tape and trace with a soft pencil.

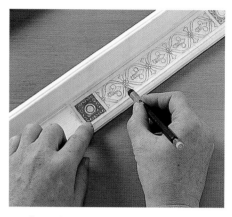

2 Place the tracing, pencil-side down, on the frame, and secure with masking tape. Using a hard pencil, draw over the design. This will transfer the pencil design on to the frame.

3 Remove the tracing paper and ink over the design with a fine black marker pen. Paint the rebate with black emulsion (latex) paint.

4 When the penwork is completed, spray clear lacquer over the frame to seal it. Wear a safety mask and hold the can approximately 20–25cm/8–10in from the frame. Leave to dry.

5 Using a flat lacquer brush, apply four layers of shellac to the frame, allowing each coat to dry for about 30 minutes before applying the next. This will give an aged, ivory appearance.

This technique involves burning a design into a frame with a heat gun. A close-grained wood, such as oak or ash, is recommended to stop the design spreading. Polish the frame with tinted wax to finish.

Scorched Frame

1 Draw your design on foil using a white chinagraph pencil. Cut out the design using a craft knife or tin snips. Place the foil template on the bare frame. Using a heat gun and wearing safety gloves, scorch the design into the wood, holding the gun 10–15cm/ 4–6in away from the wood.

2 Using coarse-grade sandpaper (glasspaper), sand off any over-burns. Repeat with fine-grade sandpaper.

3 Mix raw sienna pigment with wax in the proportion of 1.5ml/¼tsp of pigment to 15ml/1 tbsp of clear wax.

4 Apply the pigmented wax to the frame using a soft cloth. Work all around the frame.

5 Using a dry, clean cloth, polish up the wax to a soft sheen.

Tortoiseshell was popular in the eighteenth century, for hairbrush backs, trinket boxes and frames. This traditional technique, using pigments suspended in shellac over gilding, produces a realistic and effective imitation.

Tortoiseshell-effect Frame

you will need

oil paint: yellow ochre

2.5cm/1in flat oil paintbrush

wooden frame, prepared and sanded

oil size (half-hour drying time)

loose gold leaf

gilder's cushion

gilder's knife

gilder's tip

cotton wool (cotton balls)

2.5cm/1in lacquer paintbrush

pure shellac

palette or plate

pigments: yellow ochre, burnt sienna, Venetian red and burnt umber

round sable paintbrush

fine-grade wet-and-dry paper

white spirit (paint thinner)

cloths

metal polish

1 Apply yellow ochre oil paint all over the frame, and leave to dry overnight. Apply another coat and allow to dry overnight again. Apply oil size over the face and outer edges of the frame using the flat oil brush. Leave to dry for 15 minutes. When slightly tacky, begin to apply the gold leaf.

2 Place the leaf on the gilder's cushion and cut it into pieces. Brush the gilder's tip on the side of your face to pick up a little grease. Place the tip on the gold leaf and pick it up vertically. Place it on a sized section of the frame, without letting the tip touch the frame, then lift the tip up vertically. Repeat all around the frame.

3 Once the whole frame is gilded, let it dry for 20 minutes. Gently tamp down the gold leaf with cotton wool (cotton balls). Leave to dry overnight.

4 Using a lacquer brush, apply four layers of pure shellac over the frame, allowing each layer to dry for 30 minutes before applying the next. ▶

5 Mix 30ml/2 tbsp of shellac with 1.5ml/¼ tsp of yellow ochre pigment, using a round sable paintbrush. Paint this mixture on to the frame using diagonal strokes, leaving gaps for the rest of the pigments.

6 Repeat step 4. Then repeat step 5, replacing the yellow ochre pigment with burnt sienna. Apply another four layers of shellac, again allowing each to dry for 30 minutes before applying the next coat.

7 Repeat step 6 using Venetian red pigment. Apply another four layers of shellac, allowing each coat to dry completely before applying the next.

8 Repeat step 6, using burnt umber pigment. Apply eight layers of shellac, allowing each layer to dry completely before applying the next. Leave overnight.

9 When the shellac is touch dry, dip fine-grade wet-and-dry paper into a bowl of white spirit (paint thinner) and rub very gently all around the frame, ensuring that the wet-and-dry paper is saturated with white spirit. Be careful not to rub through to the pigmented layers.

10 Wipe off excess white spirit with a cloth. Then apply a small amount of metal polish and polish with another cloth to produce a smooth and shiny finish. Finally, polish the entire frame with a fresh clean cloth.

This Javanese wax-resist technique is traditionally used to produce vibrant designs in dyed fabric, but here it makes a subtle and delicate pattern on a smooth wooden picture frame.

Batik Frame

you will need

untreated wooden free-standing frame
pencil
tracing paper
ruler
general-purpose wax
wax pot or double boiler
canting
paintbrushes
woodstains: willow, mahogany and olive-green
masking tape
stencil brush (short-haired)
eraser, optional
hairdryer
cloth

1 Draw around the frame on to a piece of tracing paper and work out the design to scale, or enlarge the template provided at the back of the book. Allow for a narrow border on the inside and outside edges. Using a ruler, draw the borders on all the edges of the frame.

2 Heat the wax in a wax pot or double boiler. Wax in the ruled lines with a canting. Make sure there are no breaks in the line; the wax should stick firmly to the surface of the wood. If it brushes away easily, it is not hot enough.

3 Paint the borders with a rust-coloured woodstain, such as willow. Leave the frame to dry thoroughly.

4 Stick masking tape around the edge of the borders to protect the central frame area. ▶

5 Use a stubby stencil brush to dab wax on to the frame borders. Do not apply too much wax, as some wood must be left free of wax so that more colours can be applied.

6 Remove the masking tape. Over-paint the waxed borders with a mahogany woodstain and leave to dry completely.

7 Place the design on top of the frame and trace the leaf pattern. The pencil marks on the wood should be as light as possible. If necessary, use an eraser to remove some of the pencil.

8 Wax in the leaf design with a canting, blocking in the leaves with wax. Once again, make sure that the wax is hot enough to stick firmly to the surface of the wood.

9 Over-paint the leaf design and central area of the frame with olive-green woodstain and leave to dry.

10 When the frame is dry, heat the wax with a hairdryer until it becomes molten. Rub the molten wax into the surface of the wood with a rag. Try to spread the wax as much as possible across the surface of the frame, as this will help to bring out the colours of the woodstain.

Templates

Enlarge the templates on a photocopier. Alternatively, trace the design and draw a grid of evenly spaced squares over your tracing. Draw a larger grid on to another piece of paper and copy the outline square by square. Finally, draw over the lines to make sure they are continuous.

Painted vine mirror frame, p96

Leaf-stippled frames, p85

Framed chalkboard, pp88–89

Raised motif frame, pp86–87

Batik frame, pp123–125

Acknowledgements

The publisher would like to thank the following people for designing projects in this book:

Petra Boase for the Leaf-stippled Frames p85.
Victoria Brown for Using Decorative Mouldings pp36–37.
Stephanie Harvey for Frame Restoration pp102–103.
Alison Jenkins for the Pressed Flowerhead Frame pp105–107
Rian Kanduth for the Single-window Mount p15, Multiple-window Mount pp16–17, Stepped Mount pp18–19, Fabric-covered Mount pp20–21, Decorating a Mount: Marbled Border p24, Multi-window Frame pp46–47, Reclaimed Timber Frame pp50–51, Framing a Canvas pp54–55, Insetting Objects into a Frame pp56–57, Framing an Engraved Stone p58, Decorative Lettering p59, Cutting Glass p65, Decoupage Frame pp60–61, Lead Frame pp62–63, Colourwashed Frame

pp82–83, Raised Motif Frame pp86–87, Lime-waxed Frame p94, Woodstained Frame p95, Oil-gilded Frame pp100–101, Craquelure Frame p110, Verre Eglomisé Frame pp111–113, Ink Penwork Frame pp116–117, Scorched Frame pp118–119, Tortoiseshell Effect Frame pp120–121.
Dinah Kelly for the Crackle-glaze Picture Frame pp108–109.
Liz Wagstaff for the Gilded Shell Frame pp90–91, Good as Gold pp98–99, Water-gilded Frame pp114–115.
Stewart Walton for the Stamped Star Frame p84, Framed Chalkboard pp88–89.
Dorothy Wood for The Parts of the Frame p14, Shaped Mounts pp22–23, Decorating a Frame: Decorative lines p25, Colourwashing p25, Sponging p26, Choosing Mount Sizes p27, Securing the Artwork pp28–29, Mouldings pp30–31, Cutting and Joining a Basic Frame pp32–33, Creating a Rebate

pp34–35, Hexagonal Frame pp38–39, Halving Joint Frame pp40–41, Cross-over Frame pp42–43, Jigsaw Puzzle Frame pp44–45, Choosing Glass p64, Fitting up a Frame pp66–67, Adding Fillets p68, Hanging Pictures p69.

Thanks to the following for individual projects: Ofer Acoo, Deborah Alexander, Michael Ball, Amanda Blunden, Esther Burt, Gill Clement, Louise Gardam, Jill and David Hancock, Rachel Howard Marshall, Terry Moore, Jack Moxley, Oliver Moxley, Deborah Schneebeli-Morrell, Debbie Siniska, Karen Triffitt and Josephine Whitfield.

Thanks to the following photographers: Steve Dalton, Nicki Dowey, Rodney Forte, Michelle Garrett, Rose Jones, Debbie Patterson, Spike Powell, Graham Rae, Steve Tanner, Adrian Taylor, Lucy Tizard, Peter Williams and Polly Wreford.

Index